MILFORD
C H R O N I C L E S

MILFORD
CHRONICLES

Paul E. Curran

Edited by Maria D. Vesperi

THE
History
PRESS

Published by The History Press
Charleston, SC 29403
www.historypress.net

Front cover, top: Archer Rubber rubbers and fabrics produced in the Milford factory were shipped via Curran's Express, helmed by the author's father, John F. Curran (at left). Archer Rubber, founded in 1907, is still in business today making specialized products for the military and the aerospace industry. *Author's collection.*
Bottom: The funeral cortege of David H. Rubenstein, Milford's first World War II casualty to return home.

First published 2013

Manufactured in the United States

ISBN 978.1.62619.209.6

Library of Congress CIP data applied for.

In loving remembrance of and gratitude for my parents, John F. and Mary A. Curran, and my brothers, John Ross Curran, a man of laughter and love, and Leo Francis Curran, a man of daily courage.

CONTENTS

FOREWORD

Paul Curran had the tantalizing scraps of stories floating in his head. One concerned Mabel Bragg, who touched many lives in her classroom at Boston University and countless more with her role in creating a children's classic, *The Little Engine that Could*. Then there was the Irish Round Tower, a majestic Milford landmark and enigmatic symbol of a distant place and time. That led naturally to Father Patrick Cuddihy, the Irish priest whose 19th-century vision for his Milford flock included both the Round Tower and a "church of cathedral proportions," St. Mary's of the Assumption.

Like most people intrigued with a subject, Curran wanted the whole picture. And like most, he could tick off the names of folks who might possess those crucial details—or know someone who did.

Unlike most, however, Curran *acted* on the sense of urgency that often accompanies oral history research. There are no guarantees, of course, but most library archives stay put until someone needs them. Not so with human memory; it falters, fades and is then no more. Houses are sold and attics cleared with slight thought for their silent testimonies: a document signed with the spidery strokes of an ink-dipped pen or the faded inscription on the back of a photo. Those who do hold such legacies dear guard their treasure chests of knowledge but sometimes move elsewhere, their forwarding addresses falling gradually out of date until the trail grows cold.

Curran simply refused to let history slip through his hands. He spent countless hours on the phone, or chasing down leads in his car, or scrolling through headlines on a Microfilm reader. When letters of inquiry to far-flung sources of priceless detail went unanswered, he wrote again. While persistence was required, he found that most people were interested, even eager. Stray edges of the notes he recorded in longhand were matched against news accounts, worn pamphlets, rarely consulted books. As Curran continued to research his subjects, dozens of individuals stepped from the past, and a larger pattern came into view. He caught sight of a historical community of men and women from remarkably varied backgrounds. Their legacies were varied, too. There was "an exceptional woman and a brave one," who traveled to Appalachian classrooms in a "jolt wagon" and later taught in Constantinople and Cairo. There was the lady of the Stone Castle, who worked small miracles without leaving home. Some people lived long, influential lives; others died tragically in their youth. In life or in death, what they held in common was Milford.

"All I wanted to do was write three stories," Curran told me, "…and they just grew and grew."

Curran could have published his carefully documented research in a journal or historical magazine, but he had a different audience in mind. The broad reach and immediacy of local newspapers—perfectly archived and preserved on Microfilm—had been indispensable to his research efforts. Thus, it was fitting that he came full circle by sharing his lively tales in "Yesterdays Past," an occasional column he wrote for the *Milford Daily News* from 1996 to 2000, along with other historical features. In later years, his column moved to the *Milford Town Crier* as "Milford Moments," where it ran from 2007 to 2010.

Updated and adapted for style, "Yesterdays Past" and "Milford Moments" form the foundation of this book. A few stories included here were originally published elsewhere, and some of Curran's ongoing research appears for the first time in this volume. "A Lesson in Civics" by the late Robert Cenedella, originally featured in *American Heritage* magazine, complements Curran's perspective on an era when people were both buoyed and oppressed by complex networks of familial and social obligations. While each story stands alone as the unique record of a person, event or place, the whole is much larger. Together, they bear witness to the life of a community.

Curran brings the eye of a photographer to this project as well. The *Daily News* printed his first photographic work, and he went on to become a U.S. Army photographer in Korea and later a photojournalist in New York City. More than most, Curran recognizes that the shadow of a building and the tilt of a hat are vital elements in the construction of memories. Those who recall an earlier Main Street will view some of these photos with regret;

those who do not will regard them with wonder. Many of the oldest images preserved here would be lost to the historical record if not for Curran's efforts. The cover picture and accompanying story, which document the collective grief for a son of Milford killed in World War II, capture the essence of what *Milford Chronicles* is all about.

This volume of stories and photos is a gift to the community, one that will be just as meaningful for new residents as for those who remember open town meetings or meals and conversation at the Brass Rail. The small colonial settlement once known as the Easterly Precinct of rural Mendon drew thousands of newcomers during the Industrial Revolution, and few could forget—despite their differences—that they shared common needs, opportunities and goals.

Nowhere is this shared humanity more evident than in the description of a shop floor accident that took place at the Draper Company factory in 1882, before Hopedale was legally incorporated as a separate town. Curran bridges time to let us listen as the record of one man's death cries out for our attention: "This then was Fred Kinsley, who he was, what he was and how he died, And here, now he has lived for a few brief moments—some 130 years later—in the mind of your eye."

Curran writes with sensitivity of the class and ethnic distinctions of a bygone time, distinctions that played undeniable roles in the drama, strength and irony of Milford's history. He uses a column about an interesting landmark to offer a house-by-house census in a section of the "Plains" neighborhood, pointing out to readers: "The names reflect a social mixture of the early immigrants to that area." And later: "A wedding on Wednesday, August 12, 1896, reflects the close social nature of the early Irish and Italian neighborhood." Curran notes that the bride and groom were Italian, while the priest and an usher were Irish.

Milford Chronicles conveys the powerful if subtle pull of place that is felt by all who live in historic communities. The land itself holds memories, as Curran discovers when he learns that a boarding home fire brought death to 11 Armenian immigrants and injured many more on the very street where he played happily as a boy. He tells readers that one young man survived a month before succumbing to his injuries at Milford Hospital, a facility so overtaxed by the casualties that officials appealed to the public for bed linens. Reading this, one can begin to imagine the agony of clinging to life with severe burns back in 1914. The tragedy deepens with the knowledge that these factory workers had been warehoused 52 deep in unsafe quarters, with food so bad that 32 more had walked out just days before.

Those who left were powerless to improve the lives of those who stayed behind. But they could and did honor their dead: "The cortege was watched by hundreds as it moved through town with six of the cherry coffins arranged on a large motor truck, draped in black and covered by one large American flag, the flag of the victims' adopted country."

Written or oral, such narratives help to create what social scientists call "situated memories." My own parents, Arthur Ernest Vesperi and Mary Elizabeth (Davoren) Vesperi, were vivid storytellers who helped me to imagine trolleys on Main Street, a team of Clydesdales in the barn at the Patrick Gillon Company and heroic baseball games played and watched with a passion that still burns bright in Milford. Native Milfordians born in the first decade of the 20th century, they were blessed with an acute awareness that the pain of famine, wars and revolutions—industrial and otherwise—gave Milford its rich human texture. They took pride in the community, and they felt a sense of mutual responsibility with all who claimed it as their own.

As a child in the 1950s, I knew several Armenian elders, but I lived in carefree ignorance of their history. Then I happened to comment on one person's sad expression and another's seemingly erratic ways. Euphemisms such as "ethnic cleansing" had yet to be invented, so my father told an unvarnished tale of the Armenian massacre and its aftermath, then of the personal courage that drove these scarred but unbroken survivors to seek safety and hope in the United States—in Milford.

In the hands of a social historian, long-silent archives speak in concert with living memory. When a skillful narrator conveys those voices in the form of a vivid story, delighted readers go along for the ride. Fueled by Curran's description, even those who are new to Milford will find themselves imagining Enrico Garibaldi's blacksmith shop tucked away, "his safety glasses, his work apron, his tools, still in place from the last day that he worked there." The story of Marcia Cook may be unfamiliar, but any curious person will enjoy how Curran unwraps it: "The envelope, dirty and soiled, was postmarked Ashland, Ky., August 21, 1924, and for more than 74 years it survived in a Milford attic, its two-cent stamp still affixed." And church membership is not required to enjoy the story of the "Great Window" at St. Mary's with its lesson in human nature. In documenting that the original stained glass was destroyed in the hurricane of 1938, Curran found correspondence from a glassmaker who seemed to know his customers all too well: "If there is any possibility of finding even a small photograph of the window, we could avoid…someone remembering the old figure and not liking the new one."

"They did remember and they didn't like," Curran writes. "Two members of the class of 1939 at St. Mary's have told me that there was a lot of dissatisfaction with the window when it was finished. But time has made it acceptable."

Time smoothes the raw edges of many things, but a diminished sense of our local world is a fate we should never accept for ourselves, or for our children. Paul Curran was just 13 years old when his first photograph ran in the *Milford Daily News*, still of an age to play games on the scarred-over site of a tragic fire or to take the granite beauty of Milford's buildings as his simple due. Yet World War II was on, and he knew that the sight of soldiers on Main Street was important—maybe historic. Decades later, the same impulse to document and share prompted him to craft the newspaper stories collected here. Today, Curran worries that the weakening of local newspapers and a move away from archiving their contents will make it difficult for future generations to recapture the details of yesterdays past. "I believe strongly that 20 years from now a local historian will not be able to re-create the lives of individuals," Curran told me. "They just don't have that type of writing anymore."

Maria Davoren Vesperi
New College of Florida
August 2013

On the Photographs

Paul Curran began his life in journalism behind the camera, capturing stories as images so vivid that 70 years later, a viewer can almost feel the rumble of that tank on Main Street or his own blood being drawn by a Red Cross nurse for the war effort.

The photographs used in *Milford Chronicles* help serve the stories they tell and come from Curran's own camera, from those taken by others—a collection he's gathered over several decades—and from gifts from friends and fans of his columns on local history.

Some photographs included in this volume are not attached to a particular story but function as standalones. One shows John F. Kennedy, then campaigning for a U.S. Senate seat, visiting Milford in the 1950s, striding down Main Street, Craddock Café and the Town Hall behind him. Another features the State Theatre, a lost treasure, bustling with activity, the now vintage-era automobiles lining the street.

Photos were scanned or re-scanned to meet the publishers' specifications, and I've learned the higher the resolution, the better.

I thank Jay Sokolovsky, Noel C. Bon Tempo Sr., Jane Bigda and Josephine Anes for their assistance with scanning and archiving.

Anne Berard
Reference & Outreach Librarian
Milford Town Library

ACKNOWLEDGEMENTS

This book exists because people were willing to share their stories. I need to thank so many, but it's impossible to name them all, as memory and space prevent it. Nevertheless, I extend my gratitude to Milford and Milfordians for their support and for enduring my endless questions.

I thank Thomas Sawyer, publisher of the *Milford Daily News*, where my stories first ran as "Yesterdays Past." I also thank Brian Bodio for championing my cause.

I thank Denise Mize for our early days in journalism together.

I thank Jane Bigda, editor of the *Milford Town Crier*, where my column "Milford Moments" later appeared. She's been generous and enthusiastic as this book has come together.

I thank Maria Vesperi, friend, professor and editor, who has believed in this project for a long while. Her faith and vision have nurtured and coaxed it into being.

Anne Berard, reference librarian at the Milford Town Library, has been a determined, cheerful resource and source of support in organizing this book.

Reference Librarians Deborah Eastman and Mary Frances Best, Library Director Susan Edmonds and the entire Friends of the Milford Town Library have aided my work in thousands of ways.

Finally, I think my parents, John F. Curran and Mae Ross Curran. My father's gift for storytelling was legendary and infectious. My mother's energy and work with the American Red Cross during World War II was inspiring then, as now.

To my brothers, John Ross Curran and Leo Francis Curran, I thank you for the fun, the fights, the shenanigans and service for our country.

PAUL E. CURRAN
Milford, Ma.

FIRST PHOTO

As my years increase, so do my memories. Many faces are still vivid; others are shadows in my mind. Poet Alexander Smith wrote, "A man's real possession is his memory. In nothing else is he rich, in nothing else is he poor."

The photo shown in this chapter recently resurfaced and, with it, a few memories of Milford in the spring of 1943. In April that year, my father took me into Boston and bought me my first professional camera, a 4x5 Speed Graphic. It was secondhand and cost him $188, a lot of money then and even now. That day with him comes often now to mind, and I remember the 1940 two-door Chrysler that he drove and would drive throughout World War II and beyond.

I remember, too, that as we turned in Sherborn on Route 16 and headed toward South Natick, he slowed enough to show me where he had hidden the money for the camera. He had stuffed it down in his sock and the side of his shoe.

I'm glad I had that day with my father and that it is still a memory for me. It was a day that would influence my entire life with my introduction to photography.

A month later, the *Milford Daily News* would publish my first photograph, front page and four columns: the photo seen here. That was May 8, 1943.

The day before, as I was slowly wandering my way to St. Mary's grammar school—I was 13 and an eighth grade student—I came down Exchange Street to Main and saw the Army tank and the crowd. Somehow, I knew I had a news photo.

The location was directly in front of Cahill's News Agency and the Sears, Roebuck store. They were at 206 and 208 Main Street, and both the stores and the buildings they occupied are gone now.

World War II was in its 18th month; D-Day in Europe was more than a year away. An Army convoy passing through town was a large event, and patriotic Milfordians responded. The scene here was recorded around 8:00 a.m.

The *Daily News* reported that "in the afternoon, about 3 o'clock, three units, about 20 cars in each, of Army vehicles passed through Main Street." As word spread through the town that a convoy was coming through, spectators lined the streets and cheered and waved at the soldiers. One soldier, who was directing traffic in Lincoln Square, was besieged by children who offered him candy and other sweets. This was the Milford of 1943 with a population of 15,367.

In the photo, two Milfordians of the past are engaged in conversation with the Army officer. On the left is Charlie Darney, father to the late Fred Darney of Hopkinton and Mary—a classmate of mine at St. Mary's—who later moved to the Cape.

To the right is William L. "Bill" Power of 98 Spruce Street, a local plumber. He was the father of J. Fred Power, member of the Milford Board of Health for many years. Both are gone now.

To the right of the five children, the man in the light-colored hat is Albert "Peck" Macchi, co-owner of the Brass Rail on Central Street. Next to him is Nate Grillo, a man I knew when he worked at the Archer Rubber Co. He always called me "Camilli" in reference to the great Brooklyn Dodger first baseman; I was a devoted fan. Mr. Grillo's daughter is Reggie of Beauty Salon fame.

At the rear of the tank—on the sidewalk—the man with the cap and looking down is John F. Power, brother to Bill and also a plumber. He lived on Glines Avenue and had three sons: Andrew; Walter S., former deputy fire chief, who moved to the Cape after he retired; and John, a Hopedale resident. All have passed on since.

At the front of the tank, the man in white overalls is not identifiable.

In front of him, on the sidewalk, is John Delfino, who worked for Bill Power as a plumber and pursued an avocation as a golfer. It would become his vocation.

On the street, wearing a plaid jacket and holding a cigarette in his right hand is John Zeroogian, a native of Turkey and a familiar figure in Milford for many years. He was a moulder at Drapers and lived in Hopedale for 75 years.

The young man facing him is Bill Taylor; at least that is how I always knew him. His given name was Francis, and he grew up on Chestnut Street. For 25 years, he was a driver for Seaver's Express.

Of the five young boys in the middle, I knew the three who attended St. Mary's with me. I did not know—and could not identify personally—the tall boy on the left or the small boy on the far right.

The first boy, left, is Francis Demanche, Milford High School 1949, who later moved to Kenosha, Wisconsin. Classmate Helen Hickey Pratt identified him immediately when shown the picture, and Class President John Mazzone found him for me. Demanche passed away in May 2012.

In the white shirt and looking directly into the camera is Leo Birmingham, and over his shoulder and pointing is James Deeley. Deeley's brother Walter, St. Mary's 1947, died in Baltimore, leaving eight children. My contact in the family has not reported on James.

Leo Birmingham attended St. Mary's and as a young man was a driver for Varney Brothers Concrete. In 1962, he started the Birmingham Bus Co. and later drove for area bus companies.

The late Robert W. Griffin, the boy with the books, lived at 179 Purchase Street, but the family moved to Norton and he did not graduate with the class of 1949 at St. Mary's. He was nearly impossible to locate until I found his address on a court document at Taunton and I called him in Arkansas. Robert Griffin served as a sergeant first class in Korea and received the Bronze Star. He had five children, "12 or 13 grandchildren" and he may be seen in the Lincoln death scene in the TV movie *The Blue and the Gray*. He acted in more than 200 plays.

The small boy on the right went "lost" for this story and may have appeared only through an appeal for someone to "find" him for me. But I saw Helen Pratt again and had the photo with me, and with another look she came up quickly with his identity: Arthur Hackenson of 15 Poplar Street and, later, 314 Main Street. He subsequently resided in Upton and is now buried in St. Mary's Cemetery.

The lady on the far right and the small boy are Mrs. Lillian (Martin) Birmingham and her son, Thomas. Eighty days after the photo appeared she was a widow; her son, fatherless. Her husband, T. Joseph Birmingham, a machinist at the Draper Corp., would die on July 27, 1943, after an operation. The family lived on West Street, just before Union Street, and in 1946, Lillian Birmingham was appointed as a teacher at Stacy Jr. High School. Salary: $1,795. She retired in 1967.

Her son, Thomas J. Birmingham, would graduate from Milford High School in 1956 and Boston College in 1960. He received his MA and PhD from Princeton University and retired from the National Aeronautics and Space Administration (NASA). He lives today in Silver Springs, Md. His local relatives were the ladies Moran of Birmingham Court.

First photo—the author's first published photograph captured on May 8, 1943. *Courtesy of the author.*

A chance encounter and the tripping of a camera shutter would record a moment of Milford history and part of the cast, on one day in "Yesterdays Past." I'm glad I was a part of that day, and I know it was a day when I skipped school; the nuns never let me forget it.

FIERY FURNACE

It was a close-knit neighborhood, and we would play in the area of High, Cherry and West Maple Streets, all the way up to Meldonian's Market at 61 West Street. The Frieswick girls and brother Billy; the Slattery brothers from the top of West Street; Artie Krikorian; the Luby guys, Al and Bill, and sister Alice; Tommy Hynes; and my brothers Ross and Leo were all there. The Taxiera family (Joe Tex) and the DiNunzios were all there, too. It was our world, our neighborhood "gang."

In the winter, much of our sledding was done on High Street, when it was closed to traffic. It is this area that I write about; for it was here that the great fire of June 16, 1914, took place. It was called the "Worst Fire in Milford's History" in the headlines of the *Milford Journal* that same day.

World War I would begin in 43 days; in nine days, the Milford High School class of 1914 would graduate. But in the early hours of June 16, at West Street, Milford's holocaust would begin.

Fifty-two men went to bed that night in what was known as the Armenian boardinghouse block. A brick structure, it stood five stories high and was built by Samuel Walker as a boot factory in 1857. Converted into tenements in 1890, it dominated the landscape, extending 165 feet to the north along Cherry Street and 40 feet wide along West, similar in size to St. Mary's Church.

The fire was discovered at 2:25 a.m. as the men were awakened by the smell of smoke and the crackle of flames. The *Milford Daily Journal* reported that the "alarm was sounded from Box 35 at the corner of West and Cherry Streets, by Special [Police] Officer Ernest Bagley."

When Bagley arrived at the scene, he "found the fire alarm box the center of an excited group of the building's residents who had gotten out of the structure." According to Bagley, "They knew not how to pull the alarm." A second alarm was pulled immediately.

With the entire department responding on the double alarm, the "fire laddies placed a dozen streams of water on the building and they kept up the fight for about two hours."

The report continued: "Even while the firemen were beginning to battle with the flames which swept the upper stories, men were still jumping from windows and some…making their headway through the narrow corridors…to the street. Those who got out did so only in night clothes."

When it was all over, little remained "but the partly standing brick walls and the wreckage of the narrow stairways and corridors which state inspectors for years have allowed to prevail."

However, the state building inspector told the *Journal* reporter that "the blame rested with the officials of Milford who should have reported the facts to the state." The inspector went on to condemn local authorities "for not having reported the conditions of the buildings to the state police, if they thought it to be a fire trap." The *Journal* reported that "there is a front and rear entrance to the place, but not a fire escape or any other safeguard on the structure."

It was a disaster waiting to happen.

Reading the near century-old accounts of the fire, it is easy to imagine the scene. Images come to mind of London during World War II—from the newsreels of that time—showing figures in the dark of night fighting the fires. It must have been like that on West Street that dark and windy night.

The *Journal* reported that "there were many watching the progress of the flames, which was made gruesome by the shrieks, cries and moans of those who were inside and groping for their freedom." When the firemen began to remove the bodies of the dead, several of the survivors watched, visibly affected, and the scene was reported as "lamentable," as the "companions of the dead stood by and…shed bitter tears."

The *Milford Daily News* reported a few days after the fire that "the presence of padlocks upon the inside of some of the doors is said to be responsible for some of the deaths since in the excitement the men could not quickly unlock these appliances which were put on as an extra protection, to prevent robbery."

Of the 52 men who were living in the boardinghouse at the time of the fire, 11 would die. The *Journal* wrote that "up to last Saturday night, there had been 84 boarders and roomers in the place…but some left for reasons to do with the bill of fare provided them at meals."

Site where the West Street boardinghouse fire took place nearly 100 years ago. *Author's collection.*

Peter Topolian was the owner of 39 West Street, but it was under lease to Sarkis Chabazian, who ran the boardinghouse. Both would survive the fire, although Chabazian had to jump.

Topolian was arrested eight days after the fire and charged with having set it. State detectives from Worcester made the arrest. Arraigned before Judge Clifford A. Cook in the local court, he pleaded not guilty and was released on bail of $3,000. Topolian's bondsmen were neighbors: Hon. George F. Birch, Ex-Selectman Benjamin T. Clancy and John P. Remick, a local businessman. Dennis Shea, of Shea Bros., arrived too late at the court to participate.

Charged with "burning to defraud," Topolian was released by the grand jury sitting at Worcester, as they "found no true bills" against him.

Of the 11 Armenian men who were killed in the early morning "fiery furnace" of June 16, 1914, 10 were buried at Vernon Grove Cemetery and one at St. Mary's. As young as 22 and as old as 42, they averaged 30 years of age.

Twenty-two more were sent to Milford Hospital for treatment as a result of the fire at 39 West Street. At the scene, three doctors worked over the injured, and even now they are familiar names: Dr. Francis H. Lally, Dr.

John J. Duggan and Dr. Perry E. Joslin. Undertakers Walter W. Watson, Arthur J. Heroux and James B. Edwards were present, and before the removal of the dead, "their ambulances were used to convey the victims to the hospital."

At Milford Hospital, Supt. Emily L. Lee "called out her entire force of nurses, to battle with the unexpected conditions that faced them." The *Milford Journal* commented that "unbounded praise belongs to the doctors and nurses who did their work so incessantly." At that time, it was the largest accident case ever handled by the hospital.

Lee appealed to the public for linen, bedclothes, etc. The response was immediate and generous. The *Journal* reported that "one of the quickest and most substantial shows of interest…came from Thomas F. Flannigan of Pearl Street, who asked the *Journal* to say that the hospital could have every bit of bed linen in his home." Later, many of the burned and injured were taken to Hopedale House, a boardinghouse on Dutcher Street, and were cared for by the physicians and nurses from the hospital.

Heroes arose, and two died with the building. At a special memorial service at Trinity Episcopal Church on June 21, Rector A.J. Watson paid special tribute to Ahron Ototozzian and Aroutin Bagasian, both of whom perished in the fire while saving others in the structure. There were 125 people in attendance for the sermon, entitled "Humble Heroes of the Holocaust."

The *Journal* wrote that "beside Fireman [Michael] Burke…Fred Ruhan, another fireman, was injured and Clyde Cheney, a member of one of the hose companies was injured slightly." Burke was the most seriously injured of the firemen, cutting his left hand while making a rescue, and was treated by Dr. Joslin.

"Under all the circumstances with which they had to contend—they were working on a building which was destroying human life—the firemen did a remarkable service of good work."

On June 17, some 36 hours after they had retired for the evening at 39 West Street, the first seven victims of the fire were laid to rest at Vernon Grove Cemetery. Services were conducted at Trinity Church by Rev. Vaharene Nazaratian, pastor of the Armenian Church of Our Savior at Worcester. Then the funeral procession moved through Congress, Pine and Main Streets and on to the cemetery. The bell of Trinity Church was tolled, and the large flag on the lawn was at half-mast.

The cortege was watched by hundreds as it moved through town with six of the cherry coffins arranged on a large motor truck, draped in black and covered by one large American flag, the flag of the victims' adopted country.

Charred remains of West Street boarding house following the devastating fire in 1914. *Author's collection.*

These monuments in Vernon Grove Cemetery mark the graves of 10 men who died in the "Worst Fire in Milford's History." The 11th victim is buried in St. Mary's Cemetery. *Author's collection.*

Next came a hearse bearing the seventh coffin, and behind it, about 200 members of the Armenian colony marched.

The *Milford Daily News* reported that "respect was shown the dead by all. Places of business were closed, and groups of silent people watched the sad procession. Never before in its history has Milford witnessed such a scene as when the seven coffins passed along its Main Street and never before has the public been so touched by a local catastrophe. Sympathy in this section is universally expressed."

Burial was made in one large lot at Vernon Grove with the coffins lying side by side and the services conducted by Rev. Nazaratian. Three more victims would join the seven, two being buried with a double funeral on June 24. Finally, in July, the Armenian community would return to Vernon Grove for the burial of the tenth victim—but not the last—Simon Kaligian, widely known as "the Cook."

On July 17, the 11th and final victim, Pelibos Papaugian, age 24, would die at Milford Hospital. A Catholic, he was buried at St. Mary's Cemetery after services were conducted by the pastor, Rev. David F. McGrath.

All the expenses of the funerals, hospital and clothing for the survivors were covered by the Draper Company, where the men had worked. George A. Draper made personal calls on members of the Armenian community and gave instructions to Plant Supt. Charles Nutting "that everything be done for their relief."

The *Daily News* reported, "Mr. Draper's show of personal interest in the men…in their time of grief was evident in his visit to the scene of the calamity and it evoked much favorable comment."

The graves at Vernon Grove are marked by four stones: one for the original seven who died and then one each for the next three. At St. Mary's is the gravestone for Pilibous Paboujian (alternate spelling), the eleventh victim. It is ironic that his stone faces that of another victim, Emilio Bacchiocci, a Hopedale worker, who was shot and killed during the Draper Co. strike action in April 1913.

BLOOD BANK

Family cellars often bring forth old surprises and, in this case, an old scrapbook from World War II.

In January 1944, the Milford-Mendon Branch of the American Red Cross ran its first Red Cross Blood Bank; a second two-day drive would follow in late September. The scrapbook was kept by my mother, Mrs. John F. (Mae Ross) Curran, general chairman for the first Blood Bank, and she would serve for subsequent drives in 1944, 1945 and 1948. The Blood Banks here had great success, and they give a picture of Milford and vicinity citizens as they participated in achieving their goals.

The first Blood Bank was held in the former Elks Home at 258 Main Street, now known as Milford Commons. The *Daily News* of that time had a strong commitment to the Milford community and the small surrounding towns. As a result, the Blood Banks were given heavy publicity for their efforts. Pledge cards were available at Milford Town Hall, the *Daily News* and, at the time, four Milford banks: Milford National, Milford Federal, Home National and the Milford Savings supported the pledge card program. The latter two banks are gone now.

Although the Blood Banks in Milford seemed to have made 80 percent of their quotas, I was surprised it was not higher. The commitment by the volunteers was unusual, and many names that were listed as donors are familiar to me even now.

The photo seen in this chapter was taken during the second Blood Bank in September 1944. Salvatore (Sam) Bibbo, a cutter at the Archer Rubber Go., where he made ponchos for the war effort, came in to give a pint.

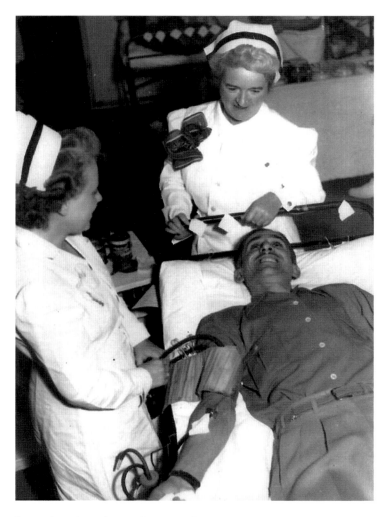

September 1944—Samuel Bibbo, 11 Genoa Avenue, makes a blood donation under the direction of Miss Jean Bedell, RN of the American Red Cross, Boston. Mrs. Charles Brisson, RN, of 54 Fruit Street, is at the head of the bed. *Courtesy of the author.*

Many others also gave blood, and in 2008, I spoke with a recipient of the Blood Bank system. Pvt. John Joseph Niro was seriously wounded in action at the Battle of St. Lo, France, on July 25, 1944. He would receive 12 pints of whole blood and 17 bottles of plasma during his 10 months in the hospital. A Milfordian from Water Street, Mr. Niro gave full credit to the blood and blood plasma that he received. He sounded strong and well when we talked, and he lived to his 87th year, passing away in late 2012. Maybe he had some Milford blood come back to him.

In January 1944, the Blood Bank raised 803 pints in three days, and the September drive collected 388 pints in two days. The Army and Navy were asking Blood Banks across the country to raise 5 million pints at that time. Milfordians gave again, and here are a few from the many: Selectman Adam Diorio and William F. Wright opened the January drive by the toss of a coin, followed by Stanley Barrows of Hopedale and Charles Goucher of Milford. And others followed: Joseph Tavano, Francis Stock, Salvatore Bufalo, Seena Heller, Gerard Lally, Nicholas Bibbo, George Bagley, Katherine Manion, Rose Guerriere, Theresa DeGesare, Grace Doherty, Regina Espanet, Daniel Doherty, Dan Gloutier, Edward Rizoli, Pomeroy Edwards and others. In 1942, Milford had a population of 15,367. It was reported, "Nearly 2000 of Milford's young people are in the service." Milford supported them throughout.

Our Irish Round Tower

Milford's Irish Round Tower, located in St. Mary's Cemetery, is a 73-foot facsimile of but one of the many towers found in Ireland today. More than 100 years old now, the tower was built in the cemetery by the fourth pastor of St. Mary's Parish, an Irish Franciscan, the Rev. Patrick Joseph Cuddihy.

Cuddihy was a builder. Before his "mission" to America in 1852, he had built churches in Ireland during his 20 years there as a priest. As a priest of the Boston diocese, he was assigned to Pittsfield and built churches in Hinsdale, Great Barrington and Lee before his assignment to the "Greater Milford Parish."

Father Cuddihy had dominated the Pittsfield scene "by sheer force of character, ability, and culture," and he would do the same in Milford for more than 41 years. In 1870, 13 years after his arrival in Milford, he completed a massive granite church—165 feet by 72 feet—with granite from his own quarry. That is the St. Mary's on Winter Street we still see today. It became Cuddihy's own tomb and memorial. He died December 8, 1898, and was buried in the ornamental stone sepulcher, finely carved, that he had placed in the foundation of the Bell Tower, the tower he added to the church in 1890.

However, before his death he had more building planned. In April 1894, the *Milford Gazette* reported that "Rev. Fr. Cuddihy had commenced work… upon the construction of a large tower in…the Catholic cemetery." This was a tower from his memory and of his youth. Irish Round Towers were in his blood; they were his heritage.

Patrick Cuddihy was born on St. Patrick's Day 1809, within the shadow of St. Patrick's Rock, Cashel, County Tipperary. He was to spend his early years there before the family returned to Clonmel, where all his siblings had been born. The Rock of Cashel—St. Patrick's Rock—rises some 300 feet "over the fertile golden vein," the rich agricultural land that surrounds it. The Irish Round Tower there rises an additional 92 feet. It is a scene not easily forgotten; it dominates the countryside for miles.

Some 85 years after his birth, Patrick Cuddihy began construction of Milford's Irish Round Tower. The memory of youth was to become a reality and a memorial to his ancestry. On October 17, 1893, Father Cuddihy visited the Boston Public Library and consulted two books: *Early Christian Architecture in Ireland* by Margaret Stokes and the definitive work on Irish Round Towers, George Petrie's *Ecclesiastical Architecture of Ireland*.

That same day, he sent a letter to the Rev. John A. Jackman, who was a former curate to Cuddihy at St. Mary's (1869), a fellow Franciscan and by then minister provincial at Dublin. It was a request for Father Jackman to buy the two books "and send them to me. I will pay you 'all' when I get there." His letter to Father Jackman was the beginning of his Irish Round Tower for his predominantly Irish parish.

Four months before, Father Cuddihy had prepared his will. In his letter he wrote, "I'm well—but think I'm feeling like a good horse after a long ride." Cuddihy was in a hurry, and six months later, tower construction was underway. As the tower rose in the spring of 1894, the new St. Mary's Cemetery east of Hamilton Street was being developed, as well as the pond adjacent to the tower.

Nearly a year later, on March 21, 1895, Timothy Kelly, "a well known young man...and a former member of the hook and ladder company in the days of its triumphs in the sporting line," became the first person to be buried in the new grounds at St. Mary's. During the last week of May, both the *Milford Gazette* and the *Milford Journal* reported that the tower was now at a height of some 50 feet and was expected to be capped off at a final height of 80 feet. In the end, it was 73 feet tall.

Father Cuddihy did live to see the completion of the Irish Round Tower, contrary to many published reports over the years. As the *Milford Gazette* reported on July 10, 1896: "But for the absence of the venerable pastor, Rev. Cuddihy in Ireland, the day would have been a memorable one in the history of the church, the original intention being to receive the bishop, confirm a large class of children, AND DEDICATE THE NEW CEMETERY AND TOWER, in conjunction with the anniversary observance."

The Irish Round Tower stands tall and proud in St. Mary's Cemetery. The only such tower in North America, it was erected in 1896 under the direction and supervision of Rev. Patrick Cuddihy, a Franciscan priest and County Tipperary, Ireland native. *Courtesy St. Mary of the Assumption Parish.*

Father Cuddihy had sailed from Boston on the *Scythia* in May 1896. It was his 14th and final trip home to his birthplace.

Five months after his death, in the *Irish Monthly* of May 1899, comes a remembrance of Father Cuddihy written by Alfred Web, an Irish biographer. Web had been on board the *Scythia* with Father Cuddihy. It is here that for the first time we have Father Cuddihy speaking of the source for his Irish Round Tower. It is not Glendalough, County Wicklow, as often assumed:

> *Seventh Day: We are making poor way against a heavy easterly swell and contrary wind. We would be lost but for Father C. He has been showing us photographs of his schools and of a round tower, modeled after that on Devenish Island, that he has built in the cemetery attached to his church.*

Webb's article is a living, vivid memory of Father Cuddihy. He called it "A Fine Old Irish Gentleman and a Good Old Priest."

Father Cuddihy has been gone now for well over a century. His tower is still with us, the only Irish Round Tower in America. The tower has gone through a major restoration, and hopefully it will stand safely for another 100 years. It was a very expensive project, and checks to support the Irish Round Tower Fund at St. Mary's Rectory came from across the United States. Special thanks should go to the three young men, Lenny Izzo Jr., Chris Keegan and Peter Pedini, who cleaned out the interior floor and to the doctor-carpenter who put up a new door. And thank you to the family of the late Thomas F. Davoren for remembering the tower in his name.

Finally, why did Father Cuddihy build the tower? His obituary in the *Clonmel* (Ireland) *Chronicle* tells the story: When chided by a friend on the subject of the tower, Father Cuddihy replied, "It may be a folly—yet when you and I have passed away the Irish in America will make a pilgrimage to the Irish Round Tower at Milford."

Folly? Five years after his death, the Wright brothers changed all that.

A Graduation Matter

High school graduation is always a special time in Milford, and it is interesting to look back 121 years to the "Graduating Exercises at Milford Music Hall on June 23, 1892." The *Oak, Lily and Ivy*, in the last issue for the class of '92, printed the program for the evening: "Miss Mary H. McDermott, Valedictory; William G. Pond, Salutatory; and the orator of the evening" was listed as Rev. Luther Freeman. The *Milford Gazette* of June 10 reported that "Rev. Freeman has accepted an invitation to deliver the baccalaureate address before the graduating class of the Milford High School."

That invitation caught the eye of Father Patrick Joseph Cuddihy, the pastor at St. Mary's, and the *Gazette* printed his objection "to having a minister of the gospel deliver an oration before the class." The *Daily News* reported that Father Cuddihy "argued that layman should be selected on these occasions and made the request that none of his congregation attend the exercises, should they be held, unless this feature was changed." It was not. The local newspapers—*Milford Gazette*, *Milford Journal* and *Daily News*—all followed the story, and it soon became known as "The High School Graduation Matter," with even the *Boston Globe* reporting on it.

The class of 1892 numbered 21—seven Protestants and 14 Catholics—with 15 of the class boys and six girls. Twenty-one graduates were scheduled for the ceremonies at Music Hall that Thursday night in June, but only six appeared to receive their diplomas. They were William G. Pond, Jessie B. Barns, Robert A. Cook, Irving C. Hill, Gertrude M. Taft and Ida S. Britton. One other student, Miss Grace Fairbanks, was unable to attend due to illness, but the next morning, Principal Chandler presented her with her MHS diploma along with a beautiful bouquet, on "behalf of the Class of '92, as a slight token of their remembrance." Nearly one year later, on June 20, 1893, at the age of 17, Miss Fairbanks died at her Congress Street home.

The 14 Catholic students had brought forth a petition and delivered it to the Milford School Committee. It was a request that Rev. Freeman be replaced as the graduation orator. The committee listened, but that was the end of it. These 14 Catholic parishioners—two-thirds of the graduates— were a gutsy group. Father Cuddihy had been in control of St. Mary's Parish for 35 years by 1892, and with time running out, a dozen or so seniors decided to appeal to their pastor the evening before the graduation.

Their pleas fell on very deaf ears, and as the *Gazette* reported, "He [Cuddihy] flatly refused to engage in reconsideration and in remarks more forcible than complimentary to those present, and threatened to excommunicate them if they dared to disobey him in the matter." Father Cuddihy evidently decided to ignore canon law, which according to the *Catholic Encyclopedia*, states that "a parish priest cannot inflict this penalty nor even declare that it is incurred."

I have studied the life of Father Cuddihy for many years, and I have had many exchanges with Ignatius Fennessy, OFM, a Franciscan priest of Killiney, Ireland. Father Ignatius is a historian and archivist and has completed a booklet on Father Cuddihy. I have learned nothing that explains the pastor's actions against the 14 innocents of the graduation class of '92.

In 1890, no public graduation exercises were held at Milford High School. In 1891, an address was delivered by Rev. A.E. Winship, and he also made the presentation of diplomas. No reaction from Father Cuddihy.

Rev. James T. Canavan was a curate to Father Cuddihy until 1898. After Father Cuddihy's death, he became the pastor until his own death in August 1904. Father Canavan was elected to the Milford School Committee in 1877 and served for nearly six years. In 1882, 10 years before "The High School Graduation Matter," the principal address at the high school graduation was delivered by Father Canavan. That fact alone makes Father Cuddihy's action more of a mystery.

Many people were hurt by the 1892 graduation but none more so than the valedictorian, Miss Mary H. McDermott, who never had her chance to deliver her talk. In November 1893, she was hired by the Milford school system and taught until 1945, retiring as a principal. Until her death in 1954, she published poetry in the *Daily News* and elsewhere.

This penny postcard features graduates similar to those of the class of 1892. *Author's collection.*

Four boys of the class became priests: Patrick Manion, John J. Rogers, Francis H. Swift and Daniel M. Tully. Robert Allen Cook became a very successful architect and a few years after graduation was hired by Father Cuddihy to design the St. Mary's (Granite) Grammar School (1895). Jesse B. Barns was the last to die of the class. That happened in 1959, and it was a long way from Milford, at Cedar Falls, Iowa. I did not learn much about his life.

I found all 21, but the last was the most difficult. Ida Sherman Briton left Milford, and I found her living and working in Providence, but then I lost track until I found her again in California. She worked in a hotel as a secretary and then, again, gone. Her burial location came to me before I found out about the end of her life and that she died in Florida. She is buried in Providence with her parents.

Charles E. Cahill, Henry D. Carbary, Mary F. Gallagher, Mrs. Fred Cahill, Katherine B. Hanly, Irving C. Hill, Fred P. Larkin, Charles J. O'Brien, Harry H. O'Connor and Stephen H. Reynolds were also members of the graduating class.

All Milfordians, but I wish that at least one, perhaps Mary Honor McDermott, had left a diary of that great "High School Graduation Matter."

A MILFORD ARTIST

On Friday, May 13, 1994, at the Annual Art Exhibit of the Milford Artists' Guild, I presented a program concerning Eunice D. Hussey, valedictorian of the Milford High School class of 1905. I offer her valedictory address here:

> *My friends—Tonight eighteen young people bid you farewell as a class. On the morrow one class of nineteen-five will take seats in the usual place. You who have been in our places can realize that. We have had our school days, and to look on the serious side, we have had some of our happiest days. Even in going farther in still higher schools, there is a difference in what will take our attention—a very great difference. And these recent bright days are not to be duplicated.*
>
> *We leave everyone of you with our thanks for your kind attention; with our teachers, volumes of gratitude. The people of the town have offered us every encouragement, and we trust that succeeding classes will prosper as well under the guidance of our efficient principal and corps of teachers. We are greatly indebted to the school committee for their careful attention to all our needs, and are especially grateful to their experienced chairman who has so generously served the many classes that have gone before. And now, once more—Farewell.*

Eunice Hussey was a Milfordian of another generation, born here in 1886. Her mother, Effie Holmes Hussey, a graduate of Milford High School, class of

1882, married local architect and builder Albertus Hussey on May 20, 1884. Both parents were born in Milford.

The early years of Eunice Hussey in Milford are vague, but in her senior year at Milford High, her writings and artwork were on display in the *Oak, Lily and Ivy*, then a monthly publication of the senior class.

At the Rhode Island School of Design, she was to meet her future husband, John Robinson Frazier, also an art student. They were married September 9, 1913. Frazier was to gain a reputation in the world of art and in 1955 became the president of the Rhode Island School of Design.

Eunice Hussey Frazier died March 27, 1926. The following is from the *Providence Journal*, found in the

Eunice Hussey Frazier posed with her son Quentin for *American Motherhood* during the summer of 1921 in Provincetown. The painting is considered the best ever produced by noted American artist Charles W. Hawthorne. *Courtesy of the Frazier Estate.*

scrapbooks the Milford Town Library staff used to keep newspaper clippings of interest to the community, a practice now long gone. The *Journal* stated:

> *Mrs. John Robinson Frazier, poetess and instructor at the Rhode Island School of Design, died yesterday morning at her home. She had been ill but a few days.*
>
> *Mrs. Frazier posed with her son Quentin, for "American Motherhood" and the painting was considered the best ever produced by artist Charles W. Hawthorne, who is considered to be one of America's foremost artists. Hawthorne died in 1930.*
>
> *She was a beautiful and charming woman, and her greatest interest lay in children and her home life. She composed a volume of children's poems,*

which were illustrated by her own drawings and published by the Oxford University Press of London [Children's Verses of the Night].

Although I have seen sketches of *Children's Verses of the Night*, Quentin Frazier has written me that he feels they are "what appears to be a draft of my mother's Book of Poems." In 1990, I made a visit to the Oxford Press but did not find any records of the poems and was informed that Oxford records were destroyed during World War II.

Eunice Hussey Frazier rests today at Lake Grove Cemetery in Holliston with her parents and her brother Clarence, a nationally known bridge and construction engineer who died in 1925.

Two lovely young women surrounded by flowers in a 1907 Rambler Runabout take part in the automobile, civic and military parade and fireman's muster for the benefit of the Milford Hospital on September 2, 1907. *Author's collection.*

Our Town Hall, with "A Lesson in Civics" by Robert Cenedella

Our Town Hall

The *Milford Daily News* of January 24, 1987, referred to Milford Town Hall as the "grand lady" of Milford. How true that is. As one local resident commented, "It is the best looking Town Hall in the Commonwealth." Undoubtedly, it is a New England classic.

The history of the Town Hall, originally called the Town House, began in 1819 when Darius and Anna Sumner gave Milford one and a half acres of land, known then as the "lower common." Today it is the site of the Town Hall. (The "upper common" is Draper Park.) A facsimile of the Sumner deed may be seen at Town Hall, near the Assessor's Office, a gift of Esther DeVita in memory of her husband, Matteo.

A "New Town House" did not come easily, but a letter to the May 13, 1853 *Milford Weekly Journal* supported the idea, saying, "Let us do something…and erect a house which shall not only witness our appreciation of Mr. Sumner's Beneficence, but tell also of our desire to provide suitable accommodations for the town in its corporate capacity."

The town delivered on the writer's request and gave us Architect Thomas W. Silloway's pristine Town Hall of 1854. Silloway was 26 when it was finished.

The exterior of the building would remain untouched until the turn of the century, when local architect Robert Allen Cook, a member of the Milford High School class of 1892, provided plans for the remodeling of

Milford Town Hall was designed by architect Thomas Silloway and later remodeled and expanded by architect Robert Allen Cook. Shown here in a 1906 photograph. *Author's collection.*

Town Hall. Cook's design added 57 feet to the rear of the building, with projecting wings on either side of the structure and an increased seating capacity of 1,500. With an ever-increasing population and open town meetings, the addition of 1900 provided badly needed space for meetings and elections. Both took place in the third-floor "Great Hall."

Inevitably, the town could not provide enough seats for its eager voters. In 1934, on a referendum question, Milford accepted "An Act establishing in the Town of Milford representative town government by limited town meetings." The act was approved by a vote of 1,536–1,170. On March 6, 1934, selectmen voted to thank the local paper and its reporter, Jacob Broudy, for presenting a series of articles on representative town government and limited meetings that offered information on both sides of the question, so residents were fully informed before they voted on the issue.

Three days later, March 9, more than 1,000 attended Annual Town Meeting—completed in one session. Just three months later, at a Special Town Meeting on June 25, there were "50 voters who were scattered throughout the large hall" as they acted on a seven-article warrant. An era in Milford history had come to an end.

The following March, elections were held in the five newly created precincts: Dewey Hall at the Town Hall; the Plains Grammar School; the Chapin Street School; the Oliver Street School; and the Park Portable School on Walnut Street.

The first Town Meeting in 1935 under the new system had 216 members from the five precincts plus 21 members-at-large for a total of 237. The five-precinct system would last for 51 years and be used for the last time on April 7, 1986, for the annual town election. A seven-precinct system began in 1987. There are eight precincts as of January 1, 2012, with 240 Town Meeting members and 24 members-at-large. The idea of using voting machines for Milford elections was first put forward in Article 28 of the 1933 Annual Town Meeting. Fifty-five years later, under former Town Clerk Joseph F. Arcudi, the electronic ballot system was put in place for the first time at the annual town election on April 4, 1988.

On September 25, 1988, Rededication Ceremonies for the Town Hall took place. A similar ceremony was held in November 1999, when a total restoration of the Great Hall was complete.

THE GREAT HALL

The late Robert Cenedella, former Milfordian, teacher, Stacy principal, writer and 1928 Milford High graduate, was a town meeting member from Precinct 1 in 1935 along with his father, Philip. Twenty-five years later, in the December 1960 issue of *American Heritage Magazine*, Cenedella published "A Lesson in Civics." It is the story of a Milford Town Meeting in the "Great Hall." It is not a memoir of his first town meeting experience in 1935 but the story of Milford's "most wondrous town meeting that ever was," when the State Police came in from Framingham and Milford had simultaneously two chiefs of police and two chairmen of the selectmen. It was 1925. The Supreme Court of Massachusetts decided it all, and Cenedella's story tells it all.

A Lesson in Civics—But Not What They Teach in School

That splendid flower of New England—the town meeting—wilts under the scrutiny of a native son.
By Robert Cenedella

The democratic tradition—or so I am told—is nowhere more splendidly exemplified than in the small New England town. There the candidates are neighbors of the voters, and the presumption of those who grew up elsewhere is that, on the first Monday in March, the honest New Englanders soberly assess the known faults and virtues of these neighbors and invariably select the most upright of men to be selectmen and highway surveyors and keepers of the pound.

As for the New England town meeting, every U.N. delegate from the Near East is sentimental about it, and Americans from Davenport, Iowa, sigh with nostalgic fondness: "Ah, if the Russians could only attend a town meeting in Massachusetts!"

Well, I feel a certain nostalgia myself for election day in old New England, and each year when March comes in like a windy candidate for the sewer commission, I too sigh for the town meeting. But what I am sighing for is something we had better not let the Russians know about at all.

Specifically, I am thinking of 1925, when I was thirteen years old. In the wake of a municipal election and the most wondrous town meeting that ever was, my father found himself one of two chairmen of selectmen in Milford, Massachusetts—though the town by-laws made it clear that there could be only one chairman. We had two chiefs of police that year too. Chief of Police O'Brien occupied the station. On the other hand, the cops took their orders from Moloney. It was very exciting. I nearly flunked Latin that year.

The big issue of the election was who would get a job out of it. I'm sorry to disappoint the nonresident lovers of quaint old New England, but that's the way it was. There were 14,000 in Milford and to serve them, the public paymaster had to shell out to a formidable number of road menders, firemen, school janitors, cops, meat inspectors, snow shovelers, substitute teachers, special constables, inspectors of wires, tree surgeons, gravediggers, librarians' assistants, and gypsy-moth controllers. Clearly, if your backward nephew had a chance at a job pouring tar into cracks in the road, you were going to vote for the man who would invest him with the overalls of that office.

My modest connection with the political campaign started in January, when first my Uncle Freddie, then various other men, singly and in committees, called at my house to urge my father to run for selectman on the Good Government ticket.

The Good Government party—called, inevitably, the Goo-goos—was the creation of my uncle, who for a couple of years had been trying to assemble a slate strong enough to beat the Citizens' Caucus party, otherwise known to us Goo-goos as The Machine.

As far as I could make out from eavesdropping on my father's callers, the trouble with The Machine was that it didn't run Italians for selectmen. At that time, the population in Milford embraced a roughly equal number of Italians, Irish and old-line Yankees. Once upon a time the Irish had struggled against the Yankees for political representation; now, through The Machine, they had achieved practically all the political representation the town had to offer, and it was the Italians' turn to knock on the door of Town Hall. This, said my father's callers, was the year when they might make it, because The Machine had not been able to take care of every Irishman in town, and the ones who hadn't got jobs were pretty sore about it. But along with two other candidates for the board of selectmen, the Goo-goos would need a strong Italian candidate, and one and all were agreed that my father was the man of the hour.

At first my father was coy. But he was an immigrant who could remember that when he was twelve years old and newly arrived on these shores, people used to hitch up their buggies every Sunday and drive past his house to gaze at an "Eyetalian" family as they might gaze at animals in a zoo. Now they wanted him to run for selectman, and it was very gratifying. He began to think of a selectman as being after all a kind of mayor. He began to think of Town Hall as City Hall. He said, "Don't worry," when my mother told him she wouldn't speak to him if he ran for office, but there was a faraway look in his eye. Through the years since then, I have always understood the presidential itch.

Finally he said he would run. My mother went right on speaking to him and cooking for him and loving him. I think she did stop speaking to certain women associated with the Citizens' Caucus Party, though.

The Machine and the Goo-goos announced their candidates at about the same time. The Machine's candidates for selectman were one Yankee, a man named Spindel, and two Irishmen: Messrs. Higgiston and Fitzsimmons. Our side had what my uncle called a "balanced slate": my father to represent Italy, Thomas Malloy to represent Eire, and an elderly man named Damon to represent America.

Of course I had right along been in favor of my father's getting into politics, and now, in my way, I got into it myself. I typed my father's speeches and newspaper advertisements; I cheerfully ran errands; and I not only attended the Goo-goo rallies in club rooms and fire stations, but I spied on the opposition at their rallies, too. From my father, I learned the word "nepotism"; he was against it. I learned that one's opponents never had an honorable reason for running for office: candidates for trustee of the public cemetery wanted to appoint themselves gravediggers, and candidates for assessor wanted to start a lucrative insurance business. At the rallies I learned the principal orator should be, not the candidate, but a lawyer, who after all could tear his spurious passions to smaller tatters than could the less practiced office-seekers. I learned that each side must refer to the opponents' lawyer-orator as "the power behind the throne." There seemed to be a rule about this. The power behind the Goo-goo throne was my Uncle Freddie, and my, didn't he catch it from the other side! At an opposition rally, I heard an ex-police chief named Murphy declare, "I point the finger of scorn at Alfred Cenedella"—and an opposition advertisement in the *Milford Daily News* read in part as follows:

> *At a rally last night, the air was permeated with vilification and abuse of the town and its people. In referring to Mr. Fitzsimmons' community service—in decorating and paying tribute at the graves of the deceased members of the G.A.R.—the brother of one of the candidates and the chief beneficiary of the "spoils system" [Uncle Freddie!] sacrilegiously called Mr. Fitzsimmons "the graveyard candidate." To stoop to this low level and verbally debauch such a sacred national observance as Memorial Day is unparalleled in the history of politics.*

When the incumbent selectman—Citizens' Caucus men, all of them—announced the list of election tellers, there was an indignant outcry from our side. Scarcely any Goo-goos at all had been appointed, and Uncle Freddie made oratorical capital of this. By now I thought I was pretty wise in the ways of politics, and I regarded this matter of the tellers as just a talking point. I got wise after the election.

Finally election day arrived.

I started early in the morning working as a courier between the spotters and the checkers. Our election headquarters were in an office in the Town Hall, and it was my duty to run from these headquarters through the corridor, out the side door, around the building, in the front door, and into the election room where two spotters were writing down the names of the voters as they arrived. I would take a list of names from them, run all the way back to headquarters, and hand it to the checkers—women who checked the names off a voting list. Then I'd do it all over again. No one ever tackled any job with more vigor. The morning vote was slow, but I was in there pitching every minute. As the newness of my duties wore off, I no longer asked the spotters for their sheets of paper: I yanked them from their hands and was gone. Once I returned to headquarters with papers I had snatched from the spotters only to have the checkers complain that there were no names at all on the papers. "Slow down, kid," one checker said, but I was halfway down the corridor.

At noon my mother phoned to say that I must come home for lunch and then go to school. High school freshmen in Milford—I was one of them— had to attend school in the afternoon, because the high school building was overcrowded. As a matter of fact, while the school situation never did generate as much excitement in the campaign as the issue of whether the chief of police should be a man named O'Brien or man named Moloney, it did get frequent mention. Everybody except a few Yankees who had no children agreed that the situation was intolerable. Both political parties declared that we should build a new school. And so we did, eleven years later.

I went home to lunch, took my schoolbooks, left the house and went straight back to my courier duties.

I continued working until eight o'clock, when the polls closed. Then my father (I suspect my mother had whispered to him) told me I had to go home. I went, because he drove me. Upstairs in the bathroom, I delivered a political speech, ending with a shadow-boxing uppercut to Higgiston's chin. Then I went to bed.

In the morning I went down to breakfast, my mother and father were already at the kitchen table, and listening to my father, I thought he had not been elected. In his vocabulary there were no genuine swear words, such as I could have taught him, but there was a word that was close to swearing: "gorramm." He used that word a lot at breakfast. Each time my mother said, "Philip!" rather automatically.

"Last year the gorramm votes were all counted by two-thirty," he said. "This year the tellers started six hours earlier—six whole gorramm hours, and still they didn't finish until three o'clock. What were they doing for six and a half extra gorramm hours?"

"Philip!" said my mother.

"*But who was elected?*" I asked.

It seemed that Higgiston of the Citizens' Caucus party had been high man and my father second. For third place on the board of selectmen, Fitzsimmons of the Citizens' Caucus had beaten my father's running mate, Malloy, by three votes. We Goo-goos had already demanded a recount.

"I've told them we shouldn't organize the new board until after the recount," my father went on, "and I've told them we should have the recount before town meeting, but will the gorrammedy fools listen to me?"

I didn't understand what town meeting had to do with it, so my father explained. The town meeting was to be held on Friday (it was now Tuesday) and two of the articles on the town warrant concerned putting the police department on civil service. If the citizens acted favorably on these articles, the policemen already holding jobs would go on civil service without examination, and they would have lifetime jobs. This included the chief of police, who was to be appointed by the new board of selectmen. At the insistence of Higgiston and Fitzsimmons, the board was to meet that very afternoon.

"And they'll appoint Moloney, and they'll hold up the recount until after town meeting and they'll try to jam civil service through, and if Malloy gets in on the recount instead of Fitzsimmons—"

In short it was a gorramm mess.

My father was right. When the selectmen met that afternoon, Higgiston and Fitzsimmons, over my father's objections, appointed Moloney chief of police, as well as a long list of other people to such offices as lockup keeper, field driver, fence viewer, burial agent, public weigher, and weigher of coal. My father joined the others in only one ballot: he voted for Higgiston to be chairman of selectmen. He regretted it later.

The recount was set for Saturday morning—the day following the town meeting. One thing could be said for this decision—it made each person in town know what he wanted. If you were a Citizens' Caucus man (and thus in favor of Moloney for chief of police), you wanted the civil service articles in the town warrant to pass on Friday night. If you were a Good Government man (and thus in favor of O'Brien), you wanted to keep these articles from coming up until the recount on Saturday; failing that you wanted the articles defeated.

There was some talk in our house about whether I should attend the town meeting. I argued that for several years our teachers had been telling us what a fine lesson in civics a town meeting was. My father asked wryly whether they were saying so this year. I was able to answer yes, that one teacher was taking a whole class to the meeting. My father said he hoped all those minors would vote against civil service. I said, well, could I go? My mother said I could if I'd promise to leave at ten o'clock. I said of course I would. My father winked at me.

On Friday night, I went early to town meeting and got a seat in the front row of the balcony. The town officials got there early, too, and so did the relatives of Moloney and O'Brien, and various politicians from surrounding towns who had the professional's academic interest in what was going to happen. There were lots of high school upperclassmen, too—and of course there were voters, though six hundred of these had to be turned away from Town Hall. By the time the meeting started there were three persons for every two seats, and the aisles were jammed.

And yet, for the first few hours the town meeting was disappointingly calm. There were no fistfights until we reached Article 13, and we didn't have to call in the state troopers until Article 14.

Article 13 concerned putting the police force, exclusive of its chief, on civil service without examination. Before Town Clerk Sullivan (Citizens' Caucus) had finished reading the article, men were popping up all over the hall, shouting "Mr. Moderator!" The moderator, a man named McLoughlin (Citizens' Caucus) recognized a man named McMahon (Citizens' Caucus), who moved to accept the article. Someone else moved an amendment to postpone action until after all the other articles in the warrant had been disposed of. The moderator made this Good Government man put his motion in writing.

There was a great debate then, often with three or four of the debaters shouting at once. My uncle spoke. A Citizens' Caucus man answered him. I couldn't hear either of them, but I cheered my uncle and booed his adversary. No one told me to shut up because everyone around me was cheering and booing too. Finally there were some shouts, and the moderator announced that the motion to postpone action was defeated. Men screamed their doubt of this. Men shouted that they hadn't known a vote was to be taken. A couple of men were struggling with each other in one of the side aisles. The moderator allowed a standing vote and appointed four or five men as tellers. I booed. The tellers announced that the motion to postpone was defeated.

So the question reverted to the original motion to accept the article. There was more debate, which I missed because I was watching a fight among the standees behind me. When I turned around, the town was voting on whether to use the check list. The tellers announced that the town rejected this. Several men moved to adjourn and were declared out of order. The moderator put McMahon's motion to accept Article 13 to a vote, and the tellers announced the result: The police were on civil service.

After that it got exciting.

There was a sort of snake dance of voters, each with his hand on the shoulder of the man in front of him, knifing through the swarms of people in the aisles. I found out afterward that these men were trying to get to the stage to announce that they doubted the vote, but the crowd was too thick—and anyhow the town clerk was reading. No one could hear him, but he must have been reading Article 14, which asked that the police chief also be put on civil service without examination.

Men were standing up yelling, "I move that we adjourn!" Others were standing up yelling, "Sit down!" The scuffling in the side aisle was getting vicious now. The space in front of the stage was filled with gesticulating, red-faced men, among them my father and my uncle. The moderator attacked his desk with the gavel. I was beating the railing in front of me and alternately shouting "Boo!" and "Hooray!" I saw a woman in the packed aisle beneath me crying.

I never did see the state troopers come in. But suddenly they were there, shouldering their way through the aisles, using their hands, pushing people, shouting at people. One trooper with a stick broke up the fight in the side aisle, and the noise subsided somewhat. There was a motion to adjourn and I could see, though I could not hear, the moderator putting it to a vote. When he declared that the motion was lost, wrangling broke out again, and the troopers had to move with renewed vigor through the crowd for another half hour or more. Finally, the moderator could be heard once more, and lo! he was announcing that sometime amid the confusion a voice vote had adopted the article. My father doubted it. He was cheered and hissed. The moderator asked his tellers to count the votes.

I don't know how the tellers determined who was standing up to vote—or which way—as distinguished from those who were standing up to fight or those who were standing up because there was no place to sit down. But they did count the votes, and they announced that Moloney was now on civil service.

There was more uproar. The Good Government adherents were doubting the vote, and the Citizens' Caucus adherents were—now—moving for adjournment. The state troopers were cheerfully shoving people toward the exits. Several people near me said, "It's all over," and I found myself part of a general push toward the out-of-doors.

Well, at least the town of Milford knew where it stood: it had a certain board of selectmen, a certain chairman of that board, and a certain chief of police, who was now protected by civil service.

This era of stability lasted twelve hours.

At the end of that period the recount had been taken, and it developed that on election day, in counting the last few hundred votes, the weary tellers had made a great number of mistakes, all of them favorable to the candidates of the Citizens' Caucus party. The recount put Fitzsimmons (Citizens' Caucus) out, and Malloy (Goo-goo) in. The new board of selectmen—the *new* new board—met immediately.

Malloy nominated my father for chairman of the board. My father seconded the nomination. Higgiston objected, saying that he had already been elected chairman by the votes of himself and my father, who were still members of the board. My father said he wouldn't have voted for Higgiston if the true result of the municipal election had been known at the time the vote was taken. The vote was illegal, he said, so it had to be taken over again by the legally elected board, and he was hereby voting for himself as chairman. Malloy jumped on the Cenedella bandwagon. Higgiston voted for Higgiston, and claimed he was still chairman.

Malloy then moved that Ernie O'Brien be appointed chief of police. Higgiston said Moloney had been made chief on Tuesday. My father said it wasn't Tuesday any longer, and that since Fitzsimmons, whose vote had put Moloney in, had not really been elected selectman, his vote was not legal. Higgiston said that Moloney had been the chief of police on Friday night when the neighborly democratic institution, the New England town meeting, had voted him the protection of civil service. My father said that Moloney could not have been police chief since the vote of a man not legally elected had given him the office, and that anyhow, the vote at town meeting had been illegal since it had been doubted by more than seven voters, and the moderator had done nothing about that. So my father and Malloy voted O'Brien in as police chief, with Higgiston voting for Moloney and maintaining that vote or no vote, Moloney *was* chief.

So the town had two chairmen of selectmen and two chiefs of police. Somehow—I never found out how—O'Brien got hold of the keys to the chief's office in Town Hall and set up shop there. Moloney moved in next door, into the office of the overseers of the poor.

Well, that was the situation in Milford in 1925, and it went on for months before the supreme court of Massachusetts decided that it was the first chairman (Higgiston) and the first chief of police (Moloney) who were legal, even though the electing board was partly illegal. The state legislature, dissatisfied with the court's decision, insured against future confusion by changing the law the way the Good Government group thought it should be changed. But that didn't help my father, who was no longer chairman.

To a thirteen-year-old boy it was not the court decision that was disenchanting—or my father's sudden slip from power. It was the fact that for

William H. Peare's drawing of Milford Town Hall, showing its glorious details and flourishes. *Author's collection.*

my elders, stopping on the Main Street sidewalk to pass the time of day with members of the opposition, the political battle seemed just a pleasant memory, like the memory of the last football season. I didn't think that was right. I thought people should crusade against evil three hundred and sixty-five days a year.

I remember very well what my father said the day he came home to announce that it was all over, that the court had dismissed the Good Government party's claims, a decision which in effect bound the town to appointments made by vote of an official who had never really been elected.

I burned with the injustice of this, but my father just smiled.

"Well," he said, "it's been a lot of fun."

That's what I learned in Massachusetts in 1925. Politicians in a democracy have too much fun. They don't seem to think that evil is really evil at all, except at election time.

I don't think it would be good to let that get around.

Originally published in American Heritage, *January 1960*
Reprinted with permission.

VOX POPULI

Debate has always been a great part of Milford's Town Meetings, and some debaters, such as J. George Cahill, Rico Ferrucci and Joe Testa, come readily to mind. They were all colorful and all outspoken. Cahill would take on anything and anyone, but it is a Joe Testa incident that is my favorite story and memory of a town meeting.

It was the Annual of 1967, and the issue was Milford's proposed dog leash law. It would go down "to a noisy defeat," as Town Meeting members were simply not "buying" a dog ban plan. But they did listen politely to all the arguments.

Rico Ferrucci led the attack on the plan and set the tone of the opposition. Joe Testa said the "worst thing" a person could do would be to tie up a dog.

Moderator John F. Curran monitored the pros and cons with icy calm, the *Daily News* reported, until Testa asked him: "Can I ask you, Mr. Moderator, are you a dog lover?"

Curran, quick at a quip, shot back: "No, no, Mr. Testa, I am not a dog lover, but I am the lover of a dog lover."

That's Town Meeting.

Today, with its eight precincts and a town meeting tradition that has closed out more than three-quarters of a century of successful local government—home rule—the list of Town Meeting members still echoes the names of the first meeting of 1935. And there are two that are symbolic of how history remembers and how history can forget.

Dominico DeTore of 36 Main Street was a Town Meeting member that first year and served for many years. A native of Italy, he was a stonecutter and worked in the Milford quarries and operated his own monument business. He died in 1969, and the special town meeting of December 15 remembered him with a resolution:

> *WHEREAS, Mr. DeTore, a member of this body from Precinct 1 from the very inception of our representative form of Town Meeting, who served long and conscientiously the citizens of Milford and*
> *WHEREAS, his love for this community and his concern for and dedication to her well-being were of a nature comparable to the famed Milford pink granite which he so magnificently carved and shaped, so do we acknowledge that in his passing the Town has lost a devoted and faithful servant.*

Daniel F. Doherty was also a charter member of that 1935 representative Town Meeting, serving from 35 West Street, Precinct 4. He would later serve

Precinct 5 from his home at 16 Westbrook Street and throughout World War II and beyond; he was a member of the Finance Committee. Mr. Doherty was the general manager of the Archer Rubber Co. "and a well known resident" at the time of his death, August 1, 1960. Ironically, his service to the town was never acknowledged in the Town Report with a resolution by Town Meeting. Daniel F. Doherty was the father of Edward Patrick Doherty, Milford's town counsel, who died on March 25, 1979. Edward "Pat" Doherty was lovingly remembered by two resolutions at the Annual Town Meeting on April 18 that year.

In a 1950 editorial, the *Milford Daily News* referred to "Annual Town Meetings…[as] a system that is probably the highest form of democracy in the world today." They are words to consider as we examine the subtle changes that are happening in contemporary times. This is the center of our government: not Town Hall but Town Meeting. It all begins with Town Meeting and Town Meeting members.

Prior to the Special Town Meeting of November 3, 1999, there were 28 vacancies in the town meeting membership, spread over six precincts. Only Precinct 7 had a full 33 members. Each year, former Town Clerk Joseph F. Arcudi would "go begging" for candidates. In 2008, after the election of April 7, the Town Meeting seats were again filled, with only one vacancy in the membership. Town Meeting seems to have moved on to a period of regeneration in numbers, but the voice of the *Daily News* from 1950 still seems very, very appropriate:

> *The debate tonight may be sharp. At times it may even border on personalities. But it won't be lofty or highfaluting. It will be right down to earth where it should be. And while government by Town Meeting continues, even in a modified form, we may hope that those citizens who would willingly surrender the duties of citizenship to all-possessive statism (state intervention in personal, social or economic matters) will finally see the errors of their ways.*

MILFORD'S OTHER
LIBRARIANS

The house of B.D. Godfrey, built by him in 1854, still stands today at the top of Pine Street—number 42 Congress Street—the home of Mr. and Mrs. Richard Buma. From that earlier household would come two of the early librarians of Wellesley College, and from that house, Melvil Dewey, the designer of the Dewey Decimal System, would be married.

Adin Ballou finished the preface of his massive *History of the Town of Milford* and dated it Hopedale, Ma., Dec. 1, 1881. On page 771 of Part II, his Biographico-Genealogical Register, he writes of the family of Benjamin Davenport Godfrey and Ann Eliza (Roberts) Godfrey and lists their children:

> *William, b. New York, Dec. 9, 1842;*
> *d. Mil., Aug 27, 1843*
> *Charles Boker, b. New York, Feb. 12, 1845*
> *m. Cora Anna Chapin, Jun. 25, 1868*
> *David Stearns, b. Boston, Feb. 29, 1848; famous musician*
> *m. Annie Donovan, 1872;*
> *Annie Roberts, b. Mil., Feb 11, 1850;*
> *m. Melville [sic] Dewey, Boston, Oct. 19, 1878.*
> *Lydia Boker, b. Mil., Aug 7, 1855; assist. high-school teacher.*

We concern ourselves here with Annie and Lydia. William had died; David Stearns Godfrey, a highly talented musician, had married and moved to Boston, although he continued to work in the Milford area, and Charles Boker Godfrey had married his high school classmate, Cora Anna Chapin, Milford High School 1862—the first class to graduate. That union would produce three children: Mabel and Grace, both of whom would graduate from Wellesley College, and Stuart C. Godfrey, West Point 1909.

Annie Roberts Godfrey, Milford High School class of 1867, had gone on to the Gannett Institute in Boston and later to Vassar College, leaving there after her junior year to become part of the opening of Wellesley College, having been selected in 1875 as the first librarian of the college by Henry F. Durant, founder.

In her book, *Apostles of Courage*, Dee Garrison writes of Annie Godfrey as "the daughter of a deeply religious shoe manufacturer whose wealth allowed her to mix socially with cultural figures like Longfellow, Lowell, and members of the Beecher family. Annie seemed a perfect match for Melvil—intelligent, well-educated, earnest, and ambitious." Twenty-five years old at the start of her Wellesley career, Annie had been married to Dewey for three years when Ballou finished his massive historical endeavor, but only the *Milford Journal* of October 23, 1878, had taken any special note of the marriage and had listed it in its columns as:

> *WEDDING OF THE WEEK—Dewey-Godfrey Nuptuals* [sic]
> *A small and informal wedding party, numbering sixty, consisting of relatives and intimate friends of the contracting parties, meet at the residence of Mr. and Mrs. B.D. Godfrey last Saturday evening, to witness the marriage of Miss Annie R. Godfrey and Mr. Melvil Dewey of Newtonville, editor of the* Library Journal, *and secretary of the American Metric Board of Boston. The ceremony was performed by Rev. O.S. Dean, and the bridal party took the late train for Newtonville, where they will reside. Refreshments were furnished by J.W. Roberts, and music by the Milford Quadrille Band. The presents were numerous, and included $250 in money. Among the guests were Richard Hoe (inventor of the Hoe printing presses) and lady, of New York, the librarian of Harvard College, and many others from out-of-town, with a few of our townspeople.*

The Rev. O.S. Dean was Rev. Oliver Stone Dean, DD, the 10th pastor of the Congregational Church who served the Milford parish from 1877 to 1883. J.W. Roberts (Joshua W.) was the "Practical" caterer and confectioner of the day, with his business located in Thayer's Block (151–159 Main Street), and he was a neighbor to the Godfreys, living at 31 Congress Street.

The Milford Quadrille Band was a popular group of the day, and their band room was also located in Thayer's Block, over Roberts' confectionery store. In early 1878, David Stearns Godfrey, Annie's brother, is listed as conducting classes in instrumental music, and he is also listed as having a quadrille band. He may well have been a member of the Milford Quadrille Band.

"The librarian of Harvard College" was Justin Winsor, who served at Harvard from 1877 to 1897 and was the first member of the American Library Association (ALA). It was Winsor, among others, who gave credit to Melvil Dewey for the birth of the American Library Association, a few months after the famous Centennial meeting at Philadelphia of the nation's librarians. Ninety men and 13 women met at Philadelphia that Centennial year, and Annie Roberts Godfrey of Milford, Ma., and Melvil Dewey of Adams Center, N.Y., were two of them.

Dee Garrison attributes the first meeting between Melvil Dewey and Annie Godfrey as having occurred in the Harvard Library shortly after his arrival in Boston from Amherst College in the spring of 1876. Dewey's own extensive diary records April 10, 1876: "Came in on the 7:40 and went at once to Harvard University Library to see John Fiske and talk with him about the Classification, etc. He was greatly interested, as was Mr. Sibley, the librarian. They made me give a lecture, as they called it, to their first assistants, and to the librarian of Wellesley College who chanced to be there."

Annie Roberts Godfrey, "who chanced to be there," was to become deeply involved with her future husband in the organization of a national association of librarians. She was one of the few women present at that Centennial year meeting from which the American Library Association was to evolve. Throughout 1876 and 1877, they were to continue an association through correspondence concerning their common library problems, and "in the latter year, she was one of a small group of American librarians who went to England to help in the inauguration there of the new Library Association of the United Kingdom." Her letters home continually refer to "Mr. Dewey," but only as "the life of the party." The courtship continued, and Garrison writes that "Annie and Melvil exchanged warm letters…their courtship marred only by the necessity for Annie to choose between Melvil and an ardent steamboat captain." Dewey prevailed though, and on October 19, 1878, at 42 Congress Street, the marriage took place.

Lydia Boker Godfrey, Milford High School 1872, attended Vassar for two years, graduating, however, from Boston University in 1878. Milford Town Reports show her teaching in the Milford school system and resigning from the high school in June 1880. She became connected with Wellesley

College in 1882 and was a member of the second class in library science ever graduated, receiving her certificate from Columbia's School of Library Economy, a school founded by her brother-in-law, Melvil Dewey. In 1893, she was appointed librarian of Wellesley College—the third of its early history—a position she held until her retirement in 1903.

The closeness of Milford's other librarians is shown again in another project of Melvil Dewey's. Fremont Rider (who married Grace Godfrey, MHS '91, Wellesley '96) writes in his 1944 volume, *Melvil Dewey*, that "Lake Placid was actually discovered" by Miss Lydia B. Godfrey, Mrs. Dewey's sister. She built a cabin on the hill overlooking Mirror Lake, near the spot that she was to occupy in summer thereafter for nearly forty years, and invited the Deweys to visit her there. They found Lake Placid's climate and scenery so delightful, and the immunity it offered from the hay fever from which they both suffered so complete, that a year later, they became her neighbors. Next to Miss Godfrey's cabin on the edge of Mirror Lake was a little run-down north-woods hotel. This ramshackle building Dewey bought. It became "the nucleus of the Lake Placid Club."

Dewey's contributions to the library world today are often overlooked, his main credited adventure being the Decimal Classification System. But he was also responsible for the first library school, his conception and creation; the American Library Association; *Library Journal*; and the Library Bureau, all common organizations of today that found Dewey the prime mover at their births. And by his side, Annie Godfrey Dewey.

From Dee Garrison:

> *Annie brought order and continuity to his life, supplementing their income during the lean years at Boston…straightening out his chaotic bookkeeping, tempering his enthusiasms, smoothing his stormy relations with others.*

From Fremont Rider:

> *Immediately they were married her influence began to show itself. She forced him to accept the hard truth that even the most utterly right of ideas is not automatically self-establishing.*
>
> *His decisions were always hers. To her he was always right. All her life this faith never wavered…even when…it was attacked…but always his work and cares came first.*

On August 3, 1922, Annie Godfrey Dewey died. Her life with Dewey had covered 44 years of unswerving loyalty in all of his undertakings. Yet she was also a pioneer in her own right and a co-founder of the American Home Economics Association, and therefore she had "every right to take pride in the flowering of her own grain of mustard seed."

Melvil Dewey was to die some nine years later on December 26, 1931. His ashes were deposited in the crypt under the altar of the beautiful Lake Placid Club chapel, beside those of Annie Godfrey Dewey and their two little grandsons.

Lydia Boker Godfrey had retired from Wellesley College in 1903, but it was hardly that for her. After several years of travel, she became enthusiastic about pottery making. When past 60, she entered the regular courses at the School of Ceramics, Alfred University, and then built and equipped a pottery studio in her home at Grand-View-on-Hudson. She contracted rheumatism, however, from working with the wet clay; this so crippled her that she had to turn to hand weaving, only to become blind. Like her sister, Annie, who was blind also at the end, she met the affliction with the same quiet Godfrey courage. She died on May 14, 1939, at Bridgeport, Conn., where she lived and worked in her final years.

Miss Grace Godfrey, niece of Annie Godfrey Dewey, had taught home economics in the Holyoke High School and at Simmons College when she was prevailed upon to become the table director at Lake Placid. She was to meet there Fremont Rider, a publisher who became interested in library work, attended library school and for many years was the head librarian at Wesleyan University. He was also the founder of the Godfrey Library of Genealogy, Middletown, Conn. The Riders were married in 1908, and Grace Godfrey Rider died on June 4, 1950.

Annie Godfrey Dewey and Melvil Dewey, the products of large families themselves, produced but one child, Godfrey Dewey. Godfrey was to grow within the profession of his parents. He received his doctor of education degree at Harvard in 1922 and served as president of Emerson College, Boston, from 1949 to 1951. Upon his death in 1977 at the age of 90, he was hailed by members of the Lake Placid Olympic Committee as "the father of winter sports in America." The president of the committee, Ron McKenzie, said, "The present 13th Winter Olympics Games was largely predicated on the sports facilities created by Dr. Dewey for the 1932 Olympics."

Lydia Godfrey's visit to a vacation cabin in 1893 had come a long, long way. The Deweys had started in Lake Placid with a simple house and five acres that grew to 400 buildings and more than 10,000 acres. And it had all started with Benjamin D. Godfrey, a man who was present in the Town Hall at the establishment of the Milford Town Library and who, on April 12, 1875, "also spoke against the removing of the library [to the Town Hall] and closed by moving that the whole matter be left with the Trustees, which was carried by a large majority."

The *Milford Gazette* reported on May 4, 1888:

> *Benjamin D. Godfrey died in Newton on April 27, 1888 and was buried at Pine Grove Cemetery, Milford. In earlier years in Milford he was one of the foremost citizens in any project calculated to be of benefit to the town, and at that time was instrumental to as great an extent, or more so perhaps, than any other resident in promoting the interests of his native town. He was thoroughly upright and honorable in all his dealings and was held in high esteem by employees and business associates and friends. Being compelled through financial reserves to give up business, he continued a resident of Milford until his removal to Newton several years ago where he has since made his home.*

And perhaps the only remembrance in Milford today of the Godfrey name is Godfrey Brook; Melvil Dewey and Annie Godfrey Dewey are gone. Their son, Godfrey Dewey, is gone too, and his two remaining survivors are childless. Yet unlike the Godfrey Brook that flows on

And on

And on,

The Godfrey line has stopped…

Paul E. Curran
"Dedication Booklet"
Milford Town Library
April 6, 1986

Author's note: This article was adapted from the "Dedication Booklet" I wrote in 1986 for the new Milford Town Library. Since the library dedication, two streets were built off West Fountain Street and named Godfrey Lane and Dewey Circle. The names were suggested by the late Seena Heller.

As to the "Godfrey line," let me quote from a letter written by the late Jeanne Godfrey Stephenson to Joanne Bird of the Town Clerk's office in 1992: "I would like to mention that page 41 does have a slight error. Just as the Godfrey Brook flows on, so does the Godfrey line! Though my Dad is

Dewey, the larger-than-life granite dog named for Dewey Decimal System inventor Melvil Dewey, celebrates all holidays at his home at the Milford Town Library. *Author's collection.*

gone (he was the only son of David Stearns Godfrey), he left two sons, five grandsons, and four great-grandsons. Not to mention all the females in the family."

Jeanne Godfrey Stephenson became a very good friend in the years since, and truly, the "Godfrey line" is very healthy, flowing and growing.

Specialty stores that once thrived under these awnings are long gone, as are the trolley tracks on Milford's Main Street, circa 1920s. *Author's collection.*

Mabel C. Bragg— Teacher, Writer

Nearly a century ago, a Boston periodical called *Something to Do: A Magazine for Boys and Girls* published "The Pony Engine" by Mabel C. Bragg. A Milford native, Bragg was born here on September 15, 1870.

At the time her story was published, she was the assistant superintendent of the Newton Public Schools and also wrote a monthly column for *Something to Do* entitled "Something to Tell." The column focused on two areas of her expertise—"storytelling" and "elocution."

It is Bragg's "Pony Engine" that was to become the catalyst for the book known throughout the world today as *The Little Engine that Could*. The story of "I Think I Can, I Think I Can" seems to enjoy both perennial and universal interest.

Some time after the story was published by Bragg in 1916, but before 1920, George H. Doran and Co., a New York publishing house, purchased the rights to "The Pony Engine." In every edition and every copy of *The Little Engine that Could*, even today, the following credit appears: From "The Pony Engine" by Mabel C. Bragg, copyrighted by George H. Doran and Co.

Actually, Doran may have never copyrighted the story. While researching the matter at the Library of Congress in Washington, I found no record of Doran's copyright. A 1994 letter from the Children's Literature Center at the Library of Congress advised me that they also "found no evidence that George C. Doran had ever copyrighted *The Little Engine that Could*." Or Bragg's "The Pony Engine," for that matter. The center added that the library's "authority in Copyright Reference said that they, too, had searched and found nothing."

The title *The Little Engine That Could* first appeared in 1920. It was a creation of a woman named Olive Beaupre Miller, editor and publisher of *My Bookhouse for Children*. Miller gives credit to Mabel Bragg and her "Pony Engine" throughout the early editions of *My Bookhouse*, but in the tenth (1926) edition, the Bragg credit is eliminated. Telling similarities remain, however.

Bragg wrote of "the Christmas toys for the children," and Miller repeats that theme in her adaptation of "The Pony Engine." While today's *Little Engine that Could* makes no mention of Christmas toys, all the dolls and toys say, "We must get over the mountain before the children awake."

On Christmas morn?

Controversy concerning its origins has surrounded *The Little Engine that Could* for many years. In 1955, 10 years after the death of Mabel Bragg, Platt and Munk, publishers of the 1930 version that we still read today, offered a cash reward of $1,000 for "authentic proof that this story theme appeared in printed form prior to 1911 and for the identity of the author beyond a reasonable doubt."

Three persons divided the $1,000 "prize" from Platt and Munk for "material relating to the origin of the story and its earliest printing." The decision as to authorship was, however, ruled "insufficient evidence." At that time, Platt and Munk had sold more than one million copies of the story and not a dollar in royalties had ever been paid to an author. An August 1990 article in *Publishers Weekly* suggests that sales may have exceeded well over eight million by that time. The book is now controlled by Grosset and Dunlap, part of the Penguin group. Penguin published an edition of *The Little Engine that Could* with new illustrations in 2005.

Regardless of her "Pony Engine" and its development into *The Little Engine that Could*, Mabel C. Bragg was an outstanding teacher and educator. After 15 years as assistant superintendent at Newton, she closed her brilliant career with 10 years as a member of the Boston University faculty. She was granted professor *emerita* status when she retired in 1940. For a number of summers, Professor Bragg taught educational methods and storytelling at Chautauqua, N.Y. She also served as a full professor for four summers at the University of Michigan School of Public Health.

I interviewed a former colleague of Mabel Bragg's at Boston University and have heard from several of her former students as well. As one person wrote, "She was such a delightful storyteller that she held her listeners spellbound whether they formed an audience at Chautauqua…or a small group of intimate friends at Pemaquid Point in Maine where in later life she spent her summers." In other words, this was a beloved teacher.

Some two weeks after the death of President Roosevelt in April 1945, Mabel Caroline Bragg died at the home of her sister in Springfield. In retirement, she resided in the Braggville section of Holliston. It could be said that she died in relative obscurity; hers was hardly a household name. Yet no one who knew or had contact with her has ever forgotten her. George Makechnie, dean *emeritus* of Sargent College and a former colleague of Mabel Bragg, recalled vividly for me the night that Mabel visited his home and recited *The Little Engine that Could* for his children.

Relative obscurity? In millions of homes throughout the country and the world, a Milford native has her name listed in a perennial children's favorite.

The late Lena E. Bragg, a relative of Mabel Bragg and a member of the Milford High School class of 1924, was philosophical about the story's ultimate authorship. As she wrote to me in 1995: "No matter what proof or origin is ever found, the 'Little Engine' is part of our life. Bless all who gave it to us."

"Hopedale's Terrible Casualty"

T he words were few. They had been torn from an old newspaper, brittle and brown, and they remained by accident. They were a part of the whole and a lingering part of the past. They read:

> ...*affliction. Also to the Hopedale Machine Company for funeral expenses, medical attendance, and the sum of $100. And especially to Mr. and Mrs. Willard, who so promptly opened their doors to our wounded and dying one. Mendon, June 21, 1882*

"Our wounded and dying one" sounded like a battle report from a war zone; the reference to the Hopedale Machine Company and to Mendon, however, made the incident—the death—a local one. But whose death and how?

A trip to the Milford Town Library and the assistance of the reference staff brought forth the *Milford Weekly Journal*—on Microfilm—for June 21, 1882, and the entire mysterious notice. "Mrs. Mary A. Kinsley returns a most grateful thanks to the employees of the Hopedale Machine Company for the sum of $423.36 received June 15th, generously contributed by them for herself and fatherless little ones, and for the many kindnesses shown her at the time of her heavy affliction."

Mary Kinsley had obviously lost her husband and her children their father. But who was he and how had he become a "wounded and dying one"?

Checking the *Journal* back through the beginning of June gave no answers, but a quick trip to the office of Milford's town clerk for a brief consultation with Joanne Bird produced a death record for Frederick R. Kinsley, who died by accident on April 27, 1882, at the age of 36 years, 11 months and two days. His occupation was listed as machinist, and he was buried in Mendon. It is to be remembered that at the time of his death, Hopedale was a village in the town of Milford; therefore, his death was recorded at Milford Town Hall. Hopedale would become a separate town almost four years later, on April 7, 1886. The *Milford Weekly Journal* for May 3, 1882, told the whole story as "Hopedale's Terrible Casualty."

Fred Kinsley had been caught in the belt webbing of the machinery that he was operating, and "his body was shockingly mangled" as he was held prisoner by the machine for some 15 seconds. Three doctors were summoned and performed the amputation of his right arm, "ether being administered, and shortly thereafter the patient was removed to the house of Mr. George Willard, just across the bridge from the machine shop." Kinsley was to die some five hours after the accident, "at 25 minutes to 9 o'clock."

His wife had arrived about six o'clock, and his two brothers were with him from the time of the accident. Fred Wheeler was there, too, a man who rode each day with Kinsley from Mendon to their work at the Hopedale Company. He was to remain until the end. Later he was to comment on "the coolness and calmness of the injured man…his chief solicitude being for his family rather than for himself." In addition to his wife, he left two young children, the youngest but 11 months old.

The funeral was held on Sunday afternoon from the Unitarian Church, Mendon, the church where his father had served as pastor. "Rev. Mr. Ballou of Hopedale assisted…Rev. Mr. Clark, pastor, in the services and each presented a becoming eulogy on the character and virtues of the departed."

Fred Kinsley was buried at Swan Dale Cemetery that afternoon, and his stone and those of his parents are visible still today. This writer found no record there of his widow or his two children.

The Mendon correspondent to the *Journal* wrote that:

> *Last Thursday…our whole community was bathed in tears when the news came…of that terrible calamity which terminated the life of Mr. Fred R. Kinsley.*
>
> *He was one of our highly esteemed neighbors—a young man of most exemplary habits, faithful in all the duties of life, kind in his disposition, quiet in his deportment, and friendly to all, which made him a particular favorite with his associates, who will not soon forget this terrible bereavement.*

Fred Kinsley's gravestone. *Author's collection.*

Words can but feebly express the agony of those torturing moments when his life became a sacrifice at the altar of his daily toil. Frugality and industry marked his career, making him beloved and useful to his family and friends. His domestic life was imbued with a love of home, and his best affections were centered around the family altar, where he leaved a disconsolate widow, with two little ones, to mourn the cruel fate and the untimely death of their dear protector.

This then was Fred Kinsley—who he was, what he was and how he died. And here, now, he has lived for a few brief moments—some 130 years later—in the mind of your eye.

Milford pink granite was discovered in 1870 by the Sherman brothers while they were on an expedition. By 1900, 1,000 men were employed at several quarries throughout Milford. It was difficult work requiring skill, strength and concentration. Workmen from Dodds Quarry are shown harvesting an enormous piece of the precious rock. *Courtesy of Robin Philbin.*

Once granite was mined, it was carved by highly skilled craftsmen who passed on their trade generation to generation. Milford pink granite can be found at the Boston Public Library, South Station, Worcester City Hall and the former Penn Station. *Author's collection.*

ENRICO GARIBALDI AND
MILFORD STREETS

In 1998, the "50 Years Ago Today" column in the *Milford Daily News* made reference to "Enrico Garibaldi" and two Milford streets, Palermo and Bologna. The streets were not familiar to me, and I had never met Enrico Garibaldi. I would learn of him, though, and of the two streets, extant today but with different names and somewhat different forms. Both streets are located off Route 109, now known as Medway Road but originally named Medway Street, and cited as such in Adin Ballou's 1882 *History of Milford*.

A lifetime resident of the "Street," Adele (Gattoni) Molinari, objects to the "Road" usage. She is most likely correct, and one may see "Street" signs in the area for Medway Street at Birch, Venice and Beaver Streets. It becomes Milford Street at the Medway line. At the end of East Main Street, at the start of Route 109, there is no street sign marked either Medway Street or Road. Not a problem for Milfordians of longevity but truly a problem for strangers.

Bologna Street became Bay Road by Town Meeting action in March 1968. Bay Road sits in a sea of streets: Venice, Turin, Naples Court and Messina. Perhaps it was named for the Bay of (at) Naples. Somehow, Bologna seemed more appropriate. The streets are located on the north side of Medway Street and northeast of Birch Street.

Things change. Palermo Str. has become Palerma Street and, by town standards and records, is not an accepted street. It is an unconnected road with a section running east from Naples Court and separated by a field in the middle.

That field has had many uses over the years and was owned by Reno Ciaramicoli. Primarily, it was used for farming as a cornfield. A Bay Road resident, Ernie Trautwein, told me that as a child growing up, he would participate in the mini-bike races that were often held there.

Joe Gattoni, a long-ago Medway Street resident, remembered Milford's semi-pro football teams that played and practiced on the field in the late 1930s and just before World War II.

The late "Tate" Bodio, our venerable sports authority, and Lou Acquafresca, athlete, both spoke of the Milford Merchants, the Milford Trojans and the Milford Town Team. A roster for a Trojans game in 1939 lists Castiglione, Grant, Luby, Rizoli, Hickey, Tusoni and Calagione. A 1940 game shows Acquafresca, Davoren and many other familiar Milford names. Some would fall on the fields of World War II.

The history of Medway Street must bring forth the name of Dominick McDavitt, who "contracted to construct the whole of it…[for] about $401.50." That was in 1835. In his *History of Milford*, Ballou refers to McDavitt as "an enterprising and venerable Irish-American citizen," for whom, "with respectful reference," Dominick Street was named by the selectmen in 1876.

McDavitt died on October 21, 1880, and the *Milford Journal* wrote of him as "the first foreigner that settled in Milford." An interesting comment.

When the selectmen named Dominick Street, they also named Middleton and Reade Streets. Along with Church Hill Street, they form a cluster of small streets on the south side of East Main Street, just beyond Cedar Street. Church Hill Street was named legally in 1941. Reade Street was named for Lawrence G. Reade, a native of Kilkenny, Ireland, and a Milford selectman in 1876. In the early 1870s, he served Milford in the General Court at Boston. Moving to Woburn for business reasons, he served there as mayor in 1905. Middleton Street was named for an early family of the Plains area, and I offer the following from the *Milford Journal* of September 1884:

> *Some years ago James Middleton bought a small home on East Main Street, in what is known as Fayville, or "Sculpintown," and instead of retaining the title, had the deed made out in the name of his sister, Catherine of New York.*
>
> *Two years ago, Middleton died, leaving no other property, and a wife and two children. No sooner does the fact become public, than Catherine claims the property and brings a writ of ejectment, which is granted after a legal fight.*

The result is that Mrs. Middleton and children have no share in the property they helped to save.

Middleton Street was also featured in an article by Jake Broudy, a *Milford Daily News* sportswriter in the '30s. In a 1936 column, Broudy wrote of Middleton Street as

> *...this brief street that houses three captains, past and present of Milford High School teams...Rap at No. 12—at feeding time—and you would find Doc Lombardi, leader of the crack 1932 team and probably the best blocking and defensive school back to play here in years.*
>
> *Push the button at No. 15 and, if you're not carrying a vacuum cleaner, you will find Marco Balzarini, captain of the '30 team, and one of the best ball carriers Milford High has had in the past decade.*
>
> *Skip a few numbers and place a small sum on No. 19. The wheel of fortune goes round and round and out comes Lou Acquafresca, newly elected captain of the 1937 grid team. Can any other street in town equal that for mass production?*

Things change. Streets change.

"At a Town Meeting holden March 2 AD 1863," it was voted to accept 73 streets in the town; today there are well over 400. At that time, Spruce Street was officially named. Prior to the 1863 vote, it was known as Chessman Street, named in August 1854 for Nathaniel Chessman.

Chessman, a minor town official, was paid $18.10 in 1848 for "returning deaths and burying poor persons." In May 1853 he was appointed by Town Meeting to the building committee "to build a new town-house upon the Common." Chessman lost his home, the "well known Chessman Estate, situated on Bear Hill, in the beautiful village of Milford," through a "Peremptory Sale" in May 1856. Many will remember it as the home of the late Dr. Frank Moschilli at 283 Central Street. A magnificent house, it was a landmark on the Bear Hill landscape. No longer to be seen, it was razed a few years ago. Nathanial Chessman's name remains, however, and may be found on the dedication plaque inside the west entrance of Milford's Town Hall.

Enrico Garibaldi was "granted a permit to erect a small blacksmith shop at the corner of Palermo and Bologna streets." That was 1948. His small blacksmith shop remained intact for more than a half century inside the small concrete block garage that he built himself. It was lovingly preserved,

Early Milford street scene. *Courtesy of Robin Philbin.*

as he last used it, by his widow, Rena, who has since passed away as well. His safety glasses, his work apron, his tools, still in place from the last day that he worked there.

MARCIA COOK—
TEACHER, TRAVELER

The envelope, dirty and soiled, was postmarked Ashland, Ky., August 21, 1924, and for more than 74 years it survived in a Milford attic, its two-cent stamp still affixed.

The letter inside reads:

> *Dear Papa,*
>
> *We arrived in Ashland about an hour ago. I met up with the others of the party on the sleeper from Washington to Ashland. There will be about ten of us going up on the train in the a.m. A Canadian girl and a Maryland young woman and Miss Underwood are the only ones who have arrived so far.*
>
> *Miss Conn, who stopped at Cleveland, is expected soon. Most of the new teachers are from Ky—about seven from the other states.*
>
> *Love,*
Marcia
>
> *P.S. Address Hindman Settlement School till I send you word of going to the other place.*

Marcia Louise Cook's letter to her "Papa"—Milford architect Robert Allen Cook (1872–1949)—reported her progress as she traveled toward the Hindman Settlement School and her second year as a teacher there.

A 1918 graduate of Milford High School, Marcia Cook received her Bachelor of Science degree from Boston University's School of Education

Future educator and traveler
Marcia Cook shown here with
her brother E. Lincoln Cook.
Courtesy of Florence Cook Shaw.

in June 1923. On August 22 of that year, she left for Kentucky and her first
year as a teacher at Hindman in what is today called Appalachia. It would be
the beginning of a lifetime adventure as a teacher and a traveler.

The sleeper from Washington to Ashland, Ky., back then was the Baltimore
and Ohio. I quote from the writing of the late Katharine Wilder of Sterling,
Ma., concerning the trip south. It is a vivid picture of what she and Marcia
Cook experienced in 1923:

> *All day we rolled across the foothills of West Virginia and the Appalachian
> range. We arrived in Ashland by nightfall and took rooms in the hotel.
> Called at an early hour, we embarked on the last stage of our train trip up
> the Big Sandy River to Lackey, the nearest railroad to Hindman.*
>
> *We were briefed that we had better wear a washable cotton dress for
> the last stage of our journey, also to wrap our suitcases in a handy piece
> of oilcloth.*
>
> *From Lackey to Hindman, we would journey via the mail hack. It was
> a jolty, rutty ride over the rock strewn creek bed. Hence, the wear and tear
> on one's suitcases was quite an issue. Oil cloth helped to keep the suitcases
> in longer wearing condition, so the older teachers had found.*
>
> *The trip from Lackey to Hindman was hot and dusty. The mail hack
> was crowded by the dozen teachers. We would meet men on horseback, and
> it seemed that they lost no chance to peer in the open sides of the two-seated
> vehicle and look over the fotched-on women as I found that we were called.*

Incidentally, the driver helped by mentioning all those who were bachelors and so forth.

We arrived in Hindman by evening, three days after I had left my home.

Marcia Cook may have been on the same train, but I have not been able to connect her to Ms. Wilder, although they were in Hindman at the same time and would have known each other in the small teaching community. Katharine Wilder's sister, Florence Wilder, had a unique perspective on this long-ago adventure. She was herself in her late 90s when she wrote to me that "nothing I have [of Katharine's] mentions any of the people whom she knew there. Hindman remained a vivid experience for her all her life."

Marcia Cook spent the school year of 1923–24 teaching the fifth grade at Hindman and returned to Milford in June 1924. That June, the *Milford Daily News* reported on her speaking engagement before the Girls' Club of the Congregational Church, where she "held her audience spellbound for nearly two hours as she told of the work among the mountaineers of Kentucky where feuds and moonshine are common, and schools and religious privileges uncommon."

Much of her talk that June and a letter in November to the Girls' Club parallel the later writings of Katharine Wilder. Marcia Cook had moved out into the countryside, "to the other place," the Quicksand School. She had moved on to "the very center of the moonshine country…in Bloody Breathitt County."

Before the Girls' Club, Marcia Cook spoke of her "school work, of her Sunday school teaching and the visits to the mountain homes. She sang hymns in the peculiar weird way the people sing them, and some of the ballads have been handed down for generations."

She went on to explain that "Hindman is miles from the railroad and is reached by a long ride in a 'jolt wagon' through the wilderness and over the 'circles' and up through the mountains."

In her letter of November 1924 to the Congregational Girls' Club, Marcia Cook gave a long, interesting view into the Kentucky countryside of nearly 90 years ago. Here are some excerpts:

It is certainly wonderful that all the young people in the Church are interested in working for us here. There are only a dozen girls in the class—we have more than twice as many boys as girls in our school. The children have no scissors, and if possible, I wish we might have some. The dolls will be just lovely, too, and will be the first that most of the girls ever had. They are all fond of crayons; pencils would be more than acceptable too. Many of them have none to use at school. They love drawing books, knives, tops, balls and harmonicas—"French harps" they call them.

I'm sure we could use the books. Most of the older children have taken a new interest in reading and it is very hopeful. The average adult has no more than a fifth grade education. They are most backward.

As old Uncle Bob Howard (a native Old Reg-Lar Baptist preacher) said at dinner the other day, "We've doless (i.e. ignorant or worthless) here. We haint never had nary chance, and a body can't do much good, no matter how much wit he has, without he has the chance."

Marcia Cook would leave the Hindman School in the spring of 1925 and move on as a teacher and a traveler. On August 28, 1926, she sailed out of New York Harbor on the SS *Lancastria* of the Cunard Line, bound for her first year at Constantinople—now Istanbul—Women's College. She would teach there until 1931.

When she arrived home in 1933, the *Milford Daily News* reported on her travels to Egypt, India and China, where "upon arriving in Peiping she was offered a position as teacher in the Peking American school." She remained there for two years.

In June 1935, she received her Master of Arts degree from Columbia and then joined the faculty of Linden Hall School—enrollment 100, faculty 24—located in Kititz, Pa. She would teach there until the summer of 1938, when she sailed for Italy, where she was married to Harlan D. Conn.

Marcia Cook had known Harlan Conn at Constantinople, and after their marriage in 1938, they would both be on the staff at the American University in Cairo (AUC). In a letter to me from Dunning S. Wilson of Los Angeles, a Near East bibliographer, Harlan Conn was put forward as "an important early figure at AUC."

In August 1964, the Conns left Egypt and came home to America, settling in Princeton, N.J. Harlan Conn would die there in December 1982. Marcia Cook Conn moved to the Kansas City, Kan. area, where her adopted son lived.

She passed away in September 1998 at age 98. She rests now in the Cook family plot at Pine Grove Cemetery, Milford, along with Harlan Conn.

She was an exceptional woman and a brave one. She wrote of the Kentucky hills that "murders are not infrequent here-abouts." Life was not easy in those hills for a young teacher in 1923. Katharine Wilder did not go back after one year in the hills, and she wrote that "my home doctor told me I came near to having…malnutrition, which was very prevalent in the mountains."

Marcia Cook went back. I wish I had known the lady.

ANDY BERNARDI—
MILFORD BASEBALL

S ome years ago, I did a number of radio shows for WMRC-AM, the Milford station, called *A Moment in Milford History*. They were very brief, and I think this is a fine way—in this column—to tell you a story that many Milfordians may have missed about a man I admired and respected, the late Andy Bernardi.

Andy was one month into his 16th year when he went down to Milford's Town Park in July 1936 to play on the Powers Post 59 of the American Legion baseball team. Coach Fred "Fitter" Cahill had arranged a tune-up game with the O'Brien Oilers, a much older group of players than the Legionnaires, "but the youngsters were thought to have the pitching and attack to give their adult rivals an evening of competition." The game drew a crowd of about 800 fans. Milford sportswriter Jake Broudy told Andy's story, and I have used it here as closely as possible:

> *Andy Bernardi, pint-sized pitcher of the Junior Legion club, provided his own opposition last evening. Thanks to the quirks of Fate, he found himself in that spot so wishfully sought by politicians—playing both sides against the middle.*
>
> *Fighting under two flags proved no obstacle for Bernardi and he struck a hopeful dollop for both causes with all the impartiality of a cop swinging a nightstick at a May Day riot. It all came about because two members of the O'Brien Oilers arrived late for their Town Park appointment. When the game time came, the Oilers, like a one-armed driver, were a hand short.*

Rather than delay the game, the Oilers borrowed Bernardi to inhabit right field. In the first frame, with one of his own mates in a scoring stance on second with two outs, Andy doused a hot smack from the bat of Joe Murray to wet down a Legion rally.

At this stage, the belated Oilers trickled into view and Andy bowed back to his own bench. Came the seventh and the Legionnaires began to water a little rally, trying to coax it into a victory.

Then up stepped Andy, now on his side of the fence, and melted down for O'Brien hot shots for a walk. When Charlie Espanet came through with a cut down the third base line, Bernardi romped in with a run, thereby experiencing the novel sensation of cutting off a run for his club in the first frame and scoring one for his mates in the last. Final score was Oilers 5, Legionnaires 3.

The preseason game that Powers Post 59 played that day listed Andy Bernardi along with some other great names from Milford's baseball history: Charlie Espanet, Johnny Casey, Joe Murray, Tom Ferguson, "Nig" DelSignore, Frank Berry, "Butch" Palma, "Horsemeat" Ferrario, Ernest Wood, Mel Graves and "Doc" DelSignore. Players from the O'Brien Oilers are harder to identify; first names were not used in the box score. Tom Davoren caught for the Oilers with "Buttonhook" Bill O'Brien as pitcher. Joe Grillo hit a triple and homer. Playing center field was Tusoni, with Gallagher at first and Pyne at second. The tardy players coming over from Hopedale were Ray Blake and Joe Leoncini. Perhaps a reader can tell us about the others, plus some first names.

Was the Legion game Andy's 15 minutes of fame? I doubt it; I think he had more than that and gave more. He never seemed to need the spotlight. His 1938 yearbook tells us that his pet aversion was: To stand before an audience, and his ambition: Sailor.

On D-Day at Omaha Beach, Andy had to face an audience, not as a sailor, but as a combat engineer facing the Germans. As an Army veteran, he was always proud of his war years.

His classmates in 1938 knew him well when they wrote, "We doubt if we shall ever forget Andy's Charlie McCarthy act. He doesn't quite measure six feet, but he has a heart of gold and a personality worth cultivating—two splendid assets." I came to know that man but hope I learn about his Charlie McCarthy act.

Milford lost a great son on February 8, 2002, and his family always remembers him best: "Your spirit, laughter and personality always lit up

Left: A young Andy Bernardi (left) in 1936 sitting next to teammate and future Nobel Prize in Physiology or Medicine laureate Dr. Joseph Murray. *Author's collection.*

Right: Andy Bernardi in more seasoned years. *Author's collection.*

the room. We miss you every day and especially in June. We honor your memories of D-Day, remember your birthday and miss you on Father's Day. Much love from your family."

Brave Midgets, champions of the 1943 Boys' Club series. *Front row*: John Verrelli, Gerald Barlow, Stanley Nale, John Covino, Bob Capuzziello. *Back row*: Arnold Votolato, co-captain; Al Consigli; Gerald, co-captain; "Camel" Comolli; Nick and Joe Graziano. *Author's collection.*

St. Mary's Windows

Some years ago, in 1995, St. Mary's Parish in Milford unveiled a beautiful booklet, "A Portrait of Faith." Written and produced by Jane Barnhart, a member of the parish, her work draws our attention to the fourteen magnificent stained-glass windows on each side of the church. These are the Marian Windows, installed by Father David F. McGrath in 1910.

They were and still are "Memorial Windows." The donors ranged from Father McGrath for a window in memory of his parents to a gift of a window by the seven children of Charles J. Smith and Mary F. (Murray) Smith in their memory. Parishioners contributed about $490 per window.

The fourteen windows were produced in Munich, Germany, by Franz Mayer and Company. The 1924 *History of St. Mary's Church* states, "These windows stand today as convincing proof of the generosity of the older generation." Words that, like the windows, still stand today.

But it is "The Great Window" of the Assumption of Mary that is of prime interest here. Again, the 1924 *History* addressed "the large and artistically wrought windows above the altar…likewise the product of Munich workmanship." Not true. Somehow, the 1924 *History* was in error on this point, and that presents a mystery.

During my research on the history of the windows, I was bothered concerning the origin of "The Great Window." An extensive search of the period September 10, 1922 (the date when Father Grace celebrated his first Mass here), through January 9, 1924 (when he announced to the parish the cost of "The Great Window"), revealed nothing.

St. Mary of the Assumption
Parish's Great Window. *Author's
collection.*

I then turned to the oral tradition of historical research: ask questions; talk to people. The answer came after I spoke with retired Milford teacher the late Dorothy M. Burns. When I inquired about "The Great Window" at St. Mary's, she explained how she had been in the church for Confirmation classes when the window was being installed during October 1923.

That information led me back to the old newspapers, where I finally discovered a brief item concerning the arrival of "The Great Window." It did not arrive from Munich but from Columbus, Ohio. A news story from September 1923 reported that "installers from the factory were expected to set it up very soon."

The 1948 parish history, *A Century at St. Mary's*, repeats the 1924 error and tells how Father Grace "replaced the sanctuary windows with Munich glass to match the other windows of the church. The large window over the altar was dedicated to St. Mary of the Assumption." But it was the Von Gerichten

Art Glass Company of Columbus that designed, produced and placed "The Great Window" in 1923.

Window thirteen in the Jane Barnhart booklet is "The Assumption of Mary into Heaven," located at the exit on the north left side of the church. It was the gift of the pastor, Father McGrath, a native of Ireland but an 1865 graduate of Milford High School. He placed the window with the simple memorial line, "Pray for the Souls of Edward and Mary McGrath."

Father McGrath's church was St. Mary's. His mother was Mary. His memorial window to his parents depicts Mary's Assumption. And it is Father McGrath's hand that is upon "The Great Window" of St. Mary's.

On January 7, 1923, Father Grace, after four months as pastor, delivered a financial report to the parish for 1922 and reported a "balance on hand of $3,633.03." It is highly unlikely he would have ordered a $4,000 stained-glass window for his new parish under those financial constraints.

The answer came when I found a great-grandson of the Von Gerichten Art Glass Company, Ted Von Gerichten of Middleton, N.J. At my request, he searched and found old company records with an order for St. Mary's, Milford, Ma., dated 1919. Father McGrath was pastor of St. Mary's until his death on December 21, 1920. "The Great Window" of St. Mary's—the Assumption of Mary—was obviously a Father McGrath project—a labor of love for this son of Ireland to his American hometown.

Firemen rescue mother and child during flash flooding in July 1938, just months before the Great Hurricane. *Author's collection.*

Severe flooding on Main Street, 1938. *Author's collection..*

THE GREAT NEW ENGLAND HURRICANE, 1938

It came without warning; it came unannounced and uninvited. It was a terrible storm. Milfordians remember it well and speak of it still today, the hurricane of Wednesday, September 21, 1938. "The Great New England Hurricane."

The *Milford Daily News* on Tuesday gave the weather forecast on the front page: "Rain tonight and probably Wednesday. Cooler tonight. Moderate northeast winds."

Reality was another matter, and Milford was "swept by a wind of hurricane force, which hit with terrifying suddenness about 4 o'clock yesterday afternoon."

The *Daily News* reported extensively on the storm in its combination edition of September 21 and 22, printed in Framingham at the plant of the *Framingham News*.

Here are some excerpts from 75 years ago:

> *The face of the town clock on the North Bow Street side of the Town Hall building was blown inside the building by the force of the wind. The other three faces remained intact and recorded the time.*
>
> *The plate glass windows in the Opera House block on the Pine and Main Street sides were the first to be blown out. The face of the Opera House clock was blown inside the building.*
>
> *The towering spire of the Congregational Church…was hurled to the ground, where it was buried point down for about six feet.*

Above: This photo taken by George Morte, a Milford High School student, shows the spire of the Congregational Church being blown to the ground by the Hurricane of '38. The spire was later replaced. *Courtesy of the Morte family.*

Left: This photo by Rita (Kellett) Hanlon was taken a few days after the Hurricane of '38. On September 21, 1938, she was in St. Mary's Church for the funeral of her father, John F. Kellett. *Courtesy of the Hanlon family.*

The front wall of the four-story building occupied by the Mullen Furniture Co., bulged and collapsed into Main Street.

Today, that is the two-story building at 208 Main Street, the former W.T. Grant store, located next to Johnny Jack's Restaurant.

Milford was placed under martial law, and the eventual results of the hurricane caused damage in excess of $1 million. My ninth birthday had recently gone by, and with the exception of an adventure with my father and brothers a few days after the hurricane, I have no lasting memories of that long-ago storm.

For years, though, I have heard—been told—that the window over the main altar of St. Mary's Church was blown out or damaged by the storm. However, while a column in the *Daily News* reported—again extensively—on the plate glass damage and repairs throughout the town, there was nothing of St. Mary's and "The Great Window."

The storm was covered for the *Daily News* by Daniel J. O'Connell—then the dean of local newspapermen—and for the *Worcester Evening Post* by James F. Smith. O'Connell was to die in 1942, and Smith went on to a long career with the Associated Press. Both men were members of St. Mary's Parish, yet nothing was written of the window. An exchange of letters with Jim Smith in the late 1990s shed no new information concerning the damage at St. Mary's.

I discovered that on July 31, 1939, ten months after the hurricane, the *Daily News* reported that "workmen commenced today repairing two windows in St. Mary's church…which were badly damaged by the hurricane of Sept. 21, [1938]."

Two windows were but a minor beginning to repairing the major damage to St. Mary's. Before it was all finished in December 1939, the glass damage alone would exceed $1,875.

Enter Wendell T. Phillips, architect and St. Mary's parishioner. Some three weeks before the *Daily News* reported on the two windows, Phillips was in touch with the Charles J. Connick Stained Glass Co., of Boston, concerning the major problem of "The Great Window" at St. Mary's.

The Phillips involvement came to my attention as the result of a chance conversation I had at the Boston Public Library in August 1996. Library researcher Joe Fullum, since retired from the BPL—a native Milfordian and 1954 St. Mary's graduate—told me of the Connick Stained Glass Archives that were available in the Fine Arts section of the library. The Connick Archives were to provide a plethora of pertinent information concerning the post-hurricane repairs at St. Mary's. They also revealed an intensity of attention extended to every detail by Architect Wendell Phillips. One letter, written to Phillips by the Connick manager, addressed the desire by Phillips "to have small rollers installed on the sill under each ventilator to prevent the ventilator rope from cutting into the sill."

I was able to copy some 55 letters, notes and sketches from the collection. I also obtained one interior photograph of the window boarded up.

The letters reveal a few interesting facts. It was originally thought that "The Great Window" had been made by Franz Mayer of Munich, as his firm had done the side windows of 1910. Not so. "The Great Window," installed in 1923, was the work of the Von Gerichten Art Glass Co. of Columbus, Ohio. (See "St. Mary's Windows," page 87.) However, Wendell Phillips wrote the Franz Mayer representatives in New York that in the "event that the window was done by the Columbus concern...we cannot do business with them, as the present Rector, Father Riordan, has had some difficulty with this firm, so under no consideration do I care to have you take this up with...Von Gerichten."

Franz Mayer of Munich received the contract to replace the center panel for $450. Replace, but not with the original design of the original company. Mayer did the work at his New York studio.

While visiting Notre Dame—his alma mater—in late July 1939, Wendell Phillips received a letter from Orin E. Skinner of the Connick Co. He wrote, "If there is any possibility of finding even a small photograph of the window, we could avoid...someone remembering the old figure and not liking the new one."

They did remember and they didn't like. Two members of the class of 1939 at St. Mary's have told me that there was a lot of dissatisfaction with the window when it was finished. But time has made it totally acceptable.

Today, three-quarters of a century later, St. Mary's still has an outstanding stained-glass window: the Great Window of the Assumption of Mary. It is also, most likely, the only one of its kind anywhere. Four-fifths Von Gerichten and one-fifth Franz Mayer. And unlike the side windows at St. Mary's, "The Great Window" was made entirely in America.

GIOVANNI BATTISTA GIACOMUZZI'S "STONE CASTLE"

Outside the town clerk's office at Milford Town Hall is a large map of Milford, circa 1898. Unfortunately, that map stops at today's Calzone Park—called back then the "Round Pond" or Basin—yet to be filled in and renamed.

However, there is a smaller map available that starts at Supple Square and continues down East Main Street to Medway Street. It may be seen at the Milford Town Library. This map shows in detail the "Plains" area of Middleton, Dominick and Reade Streets—all named in 1876—and the names of the property owners of that time.

The names reflect a social mixture of the early immigrants of that area—both Irish and Italian. They give a microcosmic view of many of the names that are found still in Milford today, but they are not necessarily found at the older, earlier locations.

Giacomo Cenedella is shown at the corner of Reade Street, facing East Main. In a few years, he will purchase from the bishop of Springfield the site of the first St. Mary's Church. At that location, Cenedella will build his stately home, later the home of Florence (Mainini) Pyne. In fact, Cenedella is shown as owning the property along East Main Street on both the east and west sides of Reade Street. The west location was his early home; the east side building he operated as a boardinghouse. The Cenedella house (west) became the early home of the Bertonazzi family.

It was the map designation for 13 Reade Street that raised my interest in the area. I knew that location as the "Stone Castle" and as the home of the late Angelina Cenedella, Angelina "Monica." (See page 129 for her story.)

"Stone Castle" is a natural name for such a magnificent-looking building, a name easily understood when one views the structure. It is also, undoubtedly, the highest structure "on the Plain." The building was constructed circa 1890, and the builder was Giovanni Battista Giacomuzzi. However, the 1898 map designation for the "Stone Castle" reads: B. AMBROSOLI, HEIRS.

Sufficient proof exists, though, to confirm that Giovanni Giacomuzzi was the builder of the "Stone Castle." Records at Worcester show that Giacomuzzi purchased the land from "Margaret Smith, wife of Patrick," dated April 9, 1889. Margaret Smith was a landowner and resident of the Dominick Street area. Her neighbors were the G. Pederzoli family. Thirteen months later, Giacomuzzi sold the land and the new building to B. Ambrosoli for $5,500.

Six years later, in September 1896, Bernardo Ambrosoli "was shot and instantly killed at Boston." Hence the map reference of 1898 to the "Ambrosoli Heirs."

Bernardo Ambrosoli was not a Milfordian, but he was "well known in Milford as proprietor of the Bear Hill Hotel and owner of considerable real estate here." The *Milford Gazette* went on to report that "Mr. Ambrosoli was in the habit of coming to Milford…and he was highly respected in the Italian colony here."

A wedding on Wednesday, August 12, 1896, reflects the close social nature of the early Irish and Italian neighborhood. At 8:00 a.m. that day, "Emma Cenedella, daughter of Giacomo Cenedella, the Italian contractor, was united in marriage to Vittorio Oliveri by Rev. Fr. James T. Canavan, at St. Mary's Church, in the presence of about 100 invited guests."

Bridesmaid was Adele Cenedella, sister of the bride, and best man was Guiseppe Pederzoli of 17 Dominick Street. Thomas McGee, neighborhood grocer and next-door neighbor to Giacomo Cenedella, was an usher along with William R. Burke. The 1900 *Milford Directory* lists Vittorio Oliveri as a stone cutter and living at 5 Reade Street. Shortly thereafter, he opened a grocery store at 121 East Main Street, the future store location of Larry Catella.

The *Milford Daily News* wrote of the wedding:

> …*After the ceremony a reception followed at the handsomely appointed residence of the bride's parents on East Main Street.*
>
> *About noon the guests were conveyed in barges and landaus—one account writes of barouches—to the St. Bernard Hotel on Beaver Street… where an elaborate wedding feast was served.*

The Stone Castle in 2013, just as regal as it was 123 years ago. *Author's collection.*

The St. Bernard Hotel of Bernardo Ambrosoli was also known as the Bear Hill Hotel. One month after the wedding—September 12—Ambrosoli was dead.

The *Milford Gazette* reported in September 1898 that the Bear Hill Hotel and the Castle, so called, were sold at public auction. The sale was to settle the estate of B. Ambrosoli.

Sixteen months later, on January 9, 1900, firebox #27 at the corner of Main and Cedar Streets was rung and the "Stone Castle" was on fire. A big fire. The cause was a defective chimney, and it was reported that "several days ago Officer Raphael Marino and Giacomo Cenedella noticed and spoke of the chimney…and feared…the danger of a fire."

The "Stone Castle" at the time of the fire was described as having "the first three stories…of stone…with a huge four gabled roof standing one and one-half stories about the stone work." The roof area was totally destroyed.

Today, as one stands before the "Stone Castle," the one-story, post-fire addition of 1900 is highly visible. Below it, both then and now, is the three-story granite castle of Giovanni Giacomuzzi, quarryman, stone mason, builder. In 2002, Phyllis Ahearn of Godfrey Lane informed me that her grandfather, Giovanni Battista Giacomuzzi, rests in a grave at Hillside Cemetery, Shrewsbury, Ma. But his monument can be seen at 13 Reade Street, Milford.

Author's note: The writer is grateful to the insight of the late Henry F. "Tate" Bodio in the preparation of this article.

ARDOLINO, BAGLEY AND JONES

On Armistice Day 1921, now called Veterans Day, the "Doughboy" statue—a World War I symbol—was dedicated at Supple Square, opposite Sacred Heart Church. The prime mover for the soldiers' monument was Charles Caruso, who came to Milford in 1884 and in June 1911 received permission "to erect a statue…in the square at the basin on East Main Street."

Caruso had originally planned to honor Christopher Columbus. In 1907, the pastor of Sacred Heart Parish, Rev. Rocco Petrarca, had petitioned selectmen to name the square for Pope Pius X. But Caruso had perseverance, and three years after the end of World War I, without a Pope or Columbus, he saw his statue, Milford's "Doughboy," put in place.

At the time of his death on July 19, 1926, Mr. Caruso was remembered "as being enthusiastic in all the war activities…and he aroused interest…in building a monument, in memory of the veterans of the World War—a fine work of art, built of granite, which he personally designed and erected."

In 1932, completion of the new concrete paving on East Main Street was seen as an opportunity to move the "Doughboy" from Supple Square to Round Pond Park. On October 8 of that year, during the Columbus Day festivities, Round Pond Park was dedicated and renamed Matthew Calzone Park "in honor of the first Milford soldier who gave his life in the World War."

In contrast to the "Doughboy," which lists the names of Milford residents who gave their lives in the Great War, the Draper Park World War I memorial tablet erected in 1939 does not include John C. Ardolino, George A. Bagley or Granville R. Jones.

On June 9, 1919, Milford held a "Welcome Home" parade for its World War I veterans. A souvenir pamphlet features a clear photograph of the wooden Honor Roll—in Draper Park—facing the post office of that day, today's police station. The 14th name is John C. Ardolini—corrected to Ardolino—and his name bears a Gold Star. The 20th name in the second row of the Honor Roll is George A. Bagley—an old Milford name—also with a Gold Star.

A 1930 photograph of the Honor Roll shows both names still in place with Gold Stars. With the exception of the "Doughboy" statue, however, the name of Granville R. Jones appears nowhere with a Gold Star.

Milford has 20 Gold Star men from World War I. Six were killed in action in France. Ten others died of disease—mainly Spanish influenza—and the remaining four died by accidents. Eight of the 20 were Milfordians by birth.

In 2002, I wrote that both Bagley and Jones are at rest in Milford. "Where Ardolino rests we do not know." Since then, I have heard from the Office of the Minister of Defense at Rome, Italy, and through the kindness of Noel C. Bon Tempo, our Renaissance doctor, I have a translation and more information on young Ardolino: "Ardolino Giovanni di Celestino…born 18 Sept. 1895, Torre le Nocelle, military district of Avellino, died 5 Sept. 1917…of wounds received in combat."

John C. Ardolino was buried in the Military Sanctuary of Redipuglia, located at Gorizia in the Friuli-Venezia Guilia region, northeast of Venice and southeast of the capital, Udine.

At the time of his death, the *Milford Daily News* wrote that "young Ardolino was well known to many here. He attended the grammar schools and then was sent by his parents back to Italy to study art at Florence," and it was there that he "was ordered to join the colors and fight for Italy." The Ardolino family name appears eight times at Redipuglia. It should appear once at Draper Park—John C. Ardolino with a Gold Star.

George A. Bagley was Regular Army; by training and commitment, he was in for the long haul. Germany had declared unrestricted submarine warfare on January 31, 1971. The United States severed relations with Germany on February 3, and George Bagley knew he would be going to war; the entire country knew it. While on duty with the Coastal Artillery Corps, he died at Fort Williams, Maine, on February 27, 1917.

Milford has had its share of Gold Star mothers. For more than 20 years, George Bagley's mother was honored as one of them. At the dedication of the

World War I granite and bronze memorial in Draper Park, on November 11, 1939, "Four Gold Star Mothers rode in an automobile in charge of Charles A. Goucher, an A.E.F. veteran," and Mrs. Hattie Bagley was one so honored.

Three months later on February 27, 1940—on the 23rd anniversary of her son's death—she would die at age 81. Her *Daily News* obituary referred to her as a Gold Star Mother and as a member of the Gold Star Mothers Association.

The name of George A. Bagley and a Gold Star should appear at Draper Park.

Granville R. Jones became a Milfordian through marriage and by his death. At St. Mary's Church, on Thanksgiving Day 1910, he married Gertrude L. Mann, daughter of Dr. Franklin W. Mann of 50 Grove Street, a successful Milford inventor. They were married by Rev. John A. McNamara, family friend and Milford native.

Eight years later on December 26, 1918, Granville R. Jones was buried with full military honors from St. Mary's, where Mass was celebrated by Rev. Fr. McNamara. At Pine Grove Cemetery, as the casket was being lowered into the grave, "Taps" were sounded by military bugler Charles V. Touhey, a familiar participant at the military funerals of that time.

The name of Granville R. Jones and a Gold Star should be placed at Draper Park.

Charles Caruso and his Soldiers' Monument Committee of 1921 had their heroes right. The "Doughboy" statue, on the front surface, "carries a palm, as a symbol of martyrs," and 21 names are listed there. Eighteen of the names appear again on the bronze plaque at Draper Park, and two names will be added with Gold Stars: Edward C. Austin and Nelson G. Maynard—today's 20.

For Memorial Day 1924, a Milford merchant, M.F. Green, placed an ad in the *Milford Daily News* that said in part, "We ask that every member of this community pause and give a thought to the mighty sacrifice of human love, ambitions and even life itself, which this Memorial Day commemorates."

The words of M.F. Green are even more poignant today as 66 Gold Stars have been added to the 20 from World War I: 55 from World War II, 5 from Korea, 6 from Vietnam.

Now, almost 90 years after Mr. Green's words were first published, three men of Milford still remain unrecognized for their "mighty sacrifice of…life itself." The time has come to add the names of Ardolino, Bagley and Jones and three Gold Stars to our Draper Park World War I monument.

Time will correct many things, but it often needs the help of the human heart.

"He's My Brother"

As a local historian in Milford, I have had a number of people contact me over the years to find lost relatives—usually deceased. Many interesting adventures and stories have emerged from the research. A few years ago, a letter arrived from Virginia—with the photo seen on the following page—and a request to explain what it was all about, if I could.

The request came from Marilyn (Miller) Oates, a 1948 graduate of St. Mary's High School and wife of the late Leo "Red" Oates, a member of the Milford High Athletic Hall of Fame since 2004.

The snapshot, as they were called in the '40s, was taken by Josephine Oates, Red's mother. She wrote on the back, "The dedication of the service flag I was telling you about, up near Davoren's." The face of the photo showed a singular date, October 1. The year was found using a perpetual calendar and a clue from the photo. It was Sunday, October 1, 1944.

The Davorens lived at 63 Pearl Street, directly across from Charles L. Fuller Square at the junction of Pearl, School, Walnut and Purchase Streets. Corporal Fuller had been killed in action during World War I, on July 20, 1918, in France. Milford selectmen named Fuller Square after him in 1922. The square still exists and is maintained by Judy Thomas of the Greenleaf Garden Club.

By 1944, the Oates family had moved to 71 School Street. It was a short walk from their home to the activities of October 1, 1944. Fortunately, on that day, Josephine Oates brought along her Kodak camera. Red was with the Marines in the South Pacific getting ready for the assault on Iwo Jima. The event of that glorious, sunny October day was based on the World War II custom in Milford of raising service flags to honor the servicemen and -women from a particular district or neighborhood in the town. On Monday, October 2, the local paper published the story "Fuller Square Service Flag Dedicated." It told much of what occurred and the people who were involved in the program; many names will still be familiar.

The flag, which had been blessed by Rev. Guy Rossi, CPS, was raised by Mrs. Umberto Tosti, the mother of four sons who were then still in the service. Donald Consoletti introduced Selectman Adam Diorio as master of ceremonies. Rev. Luther Morris, pastor of the Universalist Church, gave the

Troop 2 Scout Robert Joseph Gritte and Scoutmaster and World War I veteran William Montani raise the service flag in Fuller Square on October 1, 1944. Gritte was killed in action in Vietnam on March 4, 1967. *Courtesy of the Oates family.*

invocation. Guest speakers were Judge William A. Murray, Asst. Dist. Atty. Alfred B. Cenedella and Joseph Morcone, one of Milford's oldest citizens of Italian extraction. The Milford auxiliary police did traffic duty, the Milford Victory Band played and members of the Boy and Girl Scouts assisted during the ceremonies.

No photograph was published of the dedication, and therefore the snapshot by Mrs. Oates became the record of that day in Milford history.

The young Boy Scout and the older gentleman are never mentioned in the news story. I was able to identify the man after showing the photo to many older Milfordians. He was Edward Montani, a World War I veteran and a former Scoutmaster, who served as Boy Scout district commissioner. He was 52 when the photo was taken and died in June 1960.

The young Boy Scout was much more a mystery. I looked in the St. Mary's and Milford High yearbooks from 1947 and 1948, as I thought he and I were about the same age in 1944, but no luck. Then I went to see Babe Oliva at Oliva's Market, leaving an enlargement of the photo with him and asking if a customer might recognize the youngster. Not many days later, Babe called to say he had been showing the photo when a customer, Jean Darling, simply said, "He's my brother Robert. He was killed in Vietnam."

Robert Joseph Gritte had joined the Boy Scouts, Troop 2, in 1942. His family lived at 19 Main Street. He was killed in action in Vietnam on March 4, 1967. His Gold Star sign is located at Victor Drive and Medway Street, Milford.

By happenstance, this 1944 photo helped record the contributions of Milford residents to three wars fought by the United States.

FIRST HERO HOME:
DAVID H. RUBENSTEIN

Passover 1948. April 23, a Friday. Milford was a different town, and memory is the only connection between now and then. In New York the previous October, the first war dead buried abroad during World War II came home. Now, six months later, it was Milford's turn.

Corp. David H. Rubenstein was the 24th Milford man to lose his life in World War II. "Milford's Fallen Family" of that war would come to total 55. Rubenstein was killed in action in France on July 4, 1944. Weeks after his death, his last letter arrived home. Written on June 28 from a foxhole, it described the "carnage about him…as a slaughterhouse."

Originally buried at the United States cemetery in Blosville, France, Rubenstein's body arrived in New York aboard the *John L. McCarley* with 2,618 other "repatriated" war dead. School Supt. David I. Davoren had been appointed as chairman of the war hero reburial committee. The committee had met in February, and "it was decided…that the first body to arrive in Milford would receive the town's tribute for all of its war dead."

Rubenstein was the first to come home. The hero's body arrived via train, in Framingham, on Wednesday, April 21, 1948, and was taken to Milford's State Armory on Pearl Street.

It was reported that "Milford was in mourning…as the body of Corp. Rubenstein lay in State armory, symbolic of all Milford's war dead. The town's flags were at half staff." An honor guard, made up of Milford ex-servicemen, stood 24-hour duty at the casket until the funeral on Friday.

David Hyman Rubenstein was a member of the class of 1944 at Milford High School and, like 11 others, left school early to enter the service. The class yearbook for 1944—the 60th edition of the *Oak, Lily and Ivy*—lists Rubenstein and the military "twelve" who went away; all returned but one. They were Celso D. Trevani Jr., Louis J. Sannicandro, Joseph J. Niro, Joseph A. Gulino, George E. Warren, Thomas C. Ferretti, Michael N. Garabedian, Charles A. Grillo, Marderos Papelian, Irving J. Pearson, Herbert F. Murray and David Hyman Rubenstein.

On the evening of June 14, 1944, the parents of David Rubenstein were in the audience at John C. Lynch Auditorium and, as the *Milford Daily News* reported, "went forward as diplomas were received by parents, the graduates being absent on duty with the Armed Services." Fourteen days later, David Rubenstein wrote his last letter home; six days later he was dead.

Passover 1948. The *Milford Daily News* wrote, "Tomorrow is the beginning of Passover for the Jewish people, and the coincidence of the Milford hero's funeral being held on the same day is a tribute in itself."

The funeral cortege was small but impressive. Main Street was lined with an overflow crowd, and the children of the public and parochial schools viewed the procession and attended the religious ceremony.

A horse-drawn caisson, reported to Supt. Davoren as "the same one used in the burial rites for Franklin D. Roosevelt," carried David Rubenstein from the Armory, up Main Street and around General Draper Park, up Congress Street to Pine and down to the Pine Street synagogue. The outdoor services there were attended by a crowd estimated at some 3,000 citizens. Trailing the caisson were bearers, honorary bearers, marchers, town officials, relatives of the hero and friends.

Some names from that day, that funeral: Larry Heron, Armand J. Boucher Jr., Jake Smith, Kenneth Foye, Angelo Balzarini, Leonardo Morcone, Arthur Cozzens, John Derderian and Charles Strobeck—veterans, classmates, friends. The next day, David I. Davoren publicly thanked "each and every individual who assisted in paying respect to our World War II dead." Singled out were Ben C. Lancisi and the Milford High School band and the officers and men of Co. I, MNG.

At the synagogue, Rabbi Jona Weisbord of Milford chanted the Mourner's *Kaddish*, and the extemporaneous remarks of the eulogy were given by Rabbi Joseph S. Shubow, a chaplain in the war. The *Milford Daily News* reported his words as "heart warming" and as "stirring and appropriate tribute to the town's war dead." In his talk, Rabbi Shubow told of the greatness of America, "the only country in the world where a ceremony of this kind would so greatly be attended by those of all religions."

The funeral cortege of David H. Rubenstein, Milford's first World War II casualty to return home. The hero's body arrived via train in Framingham on Wednesday, April 21, 1948, and was taken to Milford's State Armory on Pearl Street. It was reported that "Milford was in mourning...as the body of Corp. Rubenstein lay in State armory, symbolic of all Milford's war dead. The town's flags were at half staff." An honor guard, made up of Milford ex-servicemen, stood 24-hour duty at the casket until the funeral on Friday. *Author's collection.*

Rabbi Shubow spoke of the last moments of life for David Rubenstein and of the enemy shell that killed the Milford youth and three of his fellow soldiers: "The shell wasn't discriminating, it didn't single out as its victim those of any particular religion. It was aimed at the heart of America, aimed at destroying our principles and our way of life."

What Milford lost that day will never be known, or what was lost on the days of death for 54 other Milfordians. All we can do is remember them.

David Rubenstein was buried at Beth Israel Cemetery in Everett, with full military honors. On November 8, 1948, Dr. Harry Helfand and Sidney Smith dedicated the square at Franklin and Main Streets in honor of Corp. David H. Rubenstein. His memorial marker is still in place today.

Sacred Heart and
Its Memorials

The first Mass in Milford for the Italian people was celebrated at 13 Reade Street, the "Stone Castle," in 1890. A Franciscan priest called from Boston spoke on that long-ago day of how, "In the heart of an Italian the Catholic Religion will never die. Keep up your good work and pray that some day you may have a monument in this town of which the Italians will be most proud."

On December 18, 1927, the basement church of Sacred Heart was dedicated by the Rev. Thomas M. O'Leary, bishop of the Springfield Diocese. On January 18, 1938, a banquet observed the 10th anniversary of the new Sacred Heart of Jesus Church, with more than 400 attending.

In his remarks as toastmaster, Attorney Alfred B. Cenedella stated "that the growth of the parish was reason for celebration…but plans should be considered now whereby greater strides could be made in the near future." Under Attorney Cenedella's plan, "Money would be available for a new church, or an addition to the present structure."

World War II would place any future plans on hold. But on July 20, 1947, one of the most impressive architectural buildings of Milford was dedicated: the *new* Sacred Heart of Jesus Church. Twenty years after his 1927 dedication ceremony for the lower church, Bishop Thomas M. O'Leary returned to Milford to dedicate the monumental church that we see today. Here was the church—the monument—that was prayed for in 1890 by an Italian-speaking priest from Boston's North End.

On the right side of the church entrance is the date 1927, the left side, 1946. The 1927 date represents the dedication of December 18. The year

Sacred Heart church during construction in 1946. The official re-dedication took place on July 20, 1947, officiated by Rev. Thomas O'Leary. *Author's collection.*

1946 marks the date that the new church was started on March 18 of that year. World War II had ended a short seven months before, allowing the long-delayed construction of the upper church to begin.

In his 1947 dedicatory sermon, Bishop O'Leary said, "In building this beautiful temple, the Italian people have erected not only a tower of worship for themselves, but a symbol of duty to God for everyone to see. I thank you and congratulate you."

That afternoon, 175 were confirmed by the bishop. Assisting him was Rev. Msgr. John P. Phelan, former curate at St. Mary's Parish (1901–04) and vicar general of the Springfield Diocese. The confirmation sermon was delivered by a young Rev. Charles F. Egan. Father Egan, who has since passed away, was a curate at Sacred Heart parish (1970–73 and again in 1989 until his retirement in December 1994).

Fourteen memorial windows were viewed in the new church that Dedication Day. Nine windows were donations in memory of early Milford Italians, familiar family names that are traditional at Sacred Heart parish.

Pangrazzi, DePasquale, Macchi and Zurlo memorial windows are located on the left side aisle. On the right side are windows to the memory of the Sciarillo (Sherillo), Cenedella, Morcone, Balconi and Parente families.

The five remaining windows are in memory of seven Milford men who gave their lives in World War II. Undoubtedly, these boys—sacrificed as men and aged forever from 17 to 37—would have been familiar with Sacred Heart Church in their early years.

Sebastian Bartlo Crivello was born on Memorial Day 1907 and would have known all of the early church structures of Sacred Heart except the one where he is memorialized. He was killed in action in Germany, December 11, 1944. His window is number one, right side aisle, facing the main altar.

Philip Arthur D'Alesio left Milford on March 7, 1941, with Co. I, Milford National Guard. Four years later, on March 1, 1945, he died as a result of wounds received in action against Germany. His window is number three, left side aisle.

Baldasaro (Ben) John Porzio, Milford High School, 1943, was killed in action in Belgium on January 6, 1945. An outstanding athlete, his ambition was to become an athletic coach. His window is number four, left side.

Edward Ernest Iannitelli also left Milford on March 7, 1941, with Co. I. He was "killed in battle" on June 11, 1945, in France and thus became the 17th Milford man to make the supreme sacrifice. His window is number five, left side.

Ben Porzio and Eddie Iannitelli were also side by side in life. On October 4, 1939, at the Sacred Heart Church, Eddie Iannitelli stood as sponsor to Ben Porzio at his confirmation.

The final window is number three on the right side. It honors three sons of Milford who served respectively in the Army, Army Air Corps and U.S. Navy.

Rudolph John Fino was the first Milford man reported to die in World War II. He was killed in action during the North African campaign, April 6, 1943. A Special Town Meeting in September 1945 voted to name the Pvt. Rudolph John Fino Athletic Field in his honor.

Robert Charles Frascotti was president of his 1940 class at Milford High School. He went on to Dean Academy, captained the baseball team there and joined the Army Air Corps in early 1942. He rose to the rank of first lieutenant and flew in excess of 80 missions. A member of the Eighth Air Force, he piloted a P-51 Mustang named "Umbriago." Flying on D-Day 1944, he was killed in action.

Joseph Paul Coscia was 17. He was torpedoed in the North Atlantic, November 1942, reported missing in January 1943 and declared dead December 4, 1943. He was the fifth Milford boy to give his life. The *Milford Daily News* reported that "Ralph Corey of Worcester and close friend of Coscia informed the parents that the last he saw of their son was as he was

Left: One of 14 memorial windows in Sacred Heart church. Nine are in memory of Milfordians from Italian families, and five are dedicated to Milford veterans who were killed in World War II. *Author's collection.*

Below: Sacred Heart rectory and original parochial school. *Author's collection.*

climbing into a lifeboat about to be lowered from their torpedoed ship." Corey was rescued after 15 days at sea.

Joseph Anthony DeMaria was declared missing over Indo-China in June 1945 while flying a mission as a tail gunner. Six months later—with the war over—he was declared killed in action as of July 5, 1945. For the dedication of Sacred Heart, Mr. and Mrs. Ralph DeMaria gave the gift of an altar dedicated to Mother Cabrini, in memory of their son.

This is but a part of Milford's loss in World War II; these eight men are but symbolic of all that we lost. There were 47 others.

At the North Purchase cemetery, on a small dignified headstone, is written: "Love's Last Gift—Remembrance."

May we always remember.

Author's note: While Rudolph John Fino was the first reported death, the first Milfordian to die in World War II was Chief Petty Officer Oscar A. Lundgren Jr., USN. (See "Lost at Sea, 1942," page 117.)

Girl Scout Troop 3, July 1938. *Front row*: Florence Fertitta, Kathleen Ortla, Helen Shuras, Marie Lynch and Mary Louis Luby. *Second row*: Dorothy Sears, Regina White, Ruth Baker, Avis Hubbard and Barbara Ettinger. *Third row*: Pearl Simmons, Dorothy Kaizzi, Nellie Barsamian, Josephine Tocci and Arlene Kempton. *Fourth row*: Eleanor Schultz, Elsie Boover, Concetta Celeste, Pearl Gleanon and Alta Sears. *Fifth row*: Edith Celly, Betty Frieswick, Dorothy Kennelly and Marilyn Cote. *Sixth row*: Mary Healy, Helen Wheeler, Viola Lewis and Elaine Kusmin. *Seventh row*: Patricia Dugan, Olive Frieswick, Betty Hartman, Margaret Lucchini and Lucille Newcombe. *Author's collection.*

Lost at Sea, 1942

For some time now, I have searched for a story that would focus on the Scandinavian community in Milford. Until the turn of the century, success was elusive.

In 1998—for Memorial Day—I wrote of six Milford men who died in World War II and had not received "memorial markers " in their honor. That omission has since been corrected. One of the six was Chief Petty Officer Oscar A. Lundgren Jr., USN. His marker is now in place on Cedar Street, just before Route 495. The Lundgren family home and farm was located at number 324, and even that numbered location is gone.

The Lundgrens were early Danish immigrants to America, and the family would come to include the parents, Oscar and Alma, and eight children. The sons were Charles, Oscar Jr. and William and their five sisters: Elizabeth, Signe, Lillian, Florence and Harriet—Milford High School, 1920, and a legal secretary to Judge John E. Swift.

In preparation for Memorial Day 2000 at Milford's Memorial Elementary School, teacher Jo-Ann D. Morgan contacted me for research information concerning some of our deceased veterans. Knowing her mother, Eleanor DeMaria of library fame, I dared not refuse the request, and the adventure of the search was well worth the "yes." Payment would come in the discovery of much new history of the Lundgren family and especially of Oscar Lundgren Jr. and his lifetime devotion to his father's adopted country. And in that history would come the discovery that Oscar Lundgren Jr. was the *first* Milford man to give his life in World War II.

For Memorial Day 1945, the *Milford Daily News* published photographs of the known dead, up until that date, from World War II. Oscar Lundgren's photo is there, surrounded by his fallen brothers. But the original photo had not been seen since that time. Jo-Ann Morgan needed Lundgren to complete her Memorial Day project, but where could I find that photograph from so long ago?

Oscar Lundgren was days short of his 19th birthday when he enlisted in the Navy on August 14, 1916; eight months later, America would enter World War I. He would serve in that war, the peacetime Navy and World War II until his death at sea, in the early morning hours of March 27, 1942.

At Newport, RI, on June 27, 1927, Oscar Lundgren, USN, married Mary Agnes Sullivan, a Newport resident. In May 1944, Agnes (Sullivan) Lundgren, Oscar's widow now, and their two children, a son and a daughter, were still living there. I headed for Newport. Probate records at City Hall provided the birth dates and the names of the Lundgren children and also the following: "A telegram from Rear Admiral Jacobs, Chief of the Bureau of Navigation of the US Navy, dated May 8, 1942 was presented stating that said missing absentee (Oscar A. Lundgren, Jr.) was MIA (missing in action) in the performance of his duty as a member of the Naval Force of the US."

Ironically, the editorial in the *Newport Daily News* for May 8, 1942, was titled "Overcoming U-Boats." A German submarine, *U-123*, was the instrument in the death of Oscar Lundgren and his 138 shipmates, plus the total destruction of their "Q-Ship."

Leaving Newport's City Hall, I visited the Atlantic Street area and the church where the Lundgrens were married in 1927, St. Augustine's. At the rectory, I was told that I should contact local historian Pat Murphy, an Atlantic Street resident.

Pat Murphy wasn't home when I visited, but when I rang the old-fashioned metal doorbell, his elderly mother yelled, "Come in!" We talked; she assured me that Pat would be home later and I should call him.

That evening, I called, and within minutes, Pat Murphy, a true local historian, gave me the married name and location of Oscar Lundgren's daughter, Alma. Both Oscar and his brother William had named daughters for their mother.

The next day, I spoke with Oscar's daughter Alma, and a few days later, her father's photo arrived. Jo-Ann Morgan received a copy for her Memorial Day tribute to Milford's "Fallen Family," and I also sent one along to the Italian-American Veterans for their photo display of our lost veterans.

Early in February 1942, with his family at Newport, Chief Gunner's Mate Oscar Lundgren was transferred to duty at the Portsmouth (NH) Naval Shipyard as a member of the Precommisioning Detail aboard the "Q-Ship, USS *Asterion*.

Both the *Asterion* and *Atik* were being prepared there as part of a secret operation designed for the "defense against the German submarines" that were causing havoc to Allied shipping in the Atlantic.

On the afternoon of March 23, 1942, both ships would depart Portsmouth. Shortly before sailing though, Chief Lundgren was transferred to the ill-fated *Atik*, as that ship lacked a chief gunner's mate. It would be the first and last sailing for the USS *Atik*.

Q-Ships versus U-Boats: America's Secret Project by Kenneth M. Beyer tells the story of what happened to Milford's Oscar Lundgren and his shipmates of the USS *Atik*. A portion of the book's dedication is to "The officers and men of the USS *Atik*—all killed in action."

Reinhard Hardegen, commander of the German submarine *U-123*, wrote the following of Ken Beyer's book: "A remarkable book that reveals the tragedy of a mystery ship I sunk. My sympathy is with the relatives of the brave navy men who lost their lives while fighting for their country."

The Lundgren family name is no longer a part of Milford today except in honor on Cedar Street and in stone at the North Purchase Cemetery:

1897 Oscar A. Lundgren Lost at Sea 1942

In 1941, paperboys delivered the *Evening Gazette* and the *Worcester Telegram* to Milford households. From left to right, by last name only: *Front row*: Consigli, Morin, DiAngelo, DiAngelo, Martin, Panaglin, Gritte. *Second row*: Rovedo, Murphy, Morin, Haynes, DiOrio. *Third row*: Boyd, Mancini, Parente, Hogan, Boidorian, Caputo, Panagian, Morin, Burns, Tueli, Murphy, Wellman. *Author's collection.*

MILFORD'S VERNON GROVE

In his informative article on Vernon Grove Cemetery (*Milford Daily News*, November 5, 1994), Gordon Hopper raises interesting questions concerning the history of Milford's early cemeteries and the burial practice therein. Adin Ballou, in Chapters V and XII of his massive *History of the Town of Milford*, writes of the matter in great detail. In particular he notes:

> *Our oldest burying-place has of late years received rather rough usage, especially its eastern portion. First, the whole front range of tombs were abandoned…then, large numbers of remains were removed by family relatives and others to Vernon Grove Cemetery or elsewhere, and the ground left in a broken condition. Afterwards, with or without town permission, large quantities of earth were carted away for various purposes, in some cases paying too little respect to the bones and ashes of the dead. Should all the remains of the dead be removed, and the land become salable real estate, a valuable property will fall to the Town.*

In Chapter V, Ballou writes, "This first and only cemetery of the precinct never received very extraordinary attention…or even necessary care. *Such was not then the fashion*" (italics mine).

That "valuable property" at the corner of School and Spruce Streets became the site of Milford's Memorial Hall and, in 1895, the Spruce Street School. Today we see the Milford Town Library there.

Mr. Hopper has given us an outstanding inventory of the early gravestones that are now at Vernon Grove. Much of the information recorded in this inventory may be checked against Ballou's Biographic-Genealogical Record in his *History*. Two of the names are of particular interest to this writer.

The Hopper Inventory lists Ellen Frost, 1778; Rev. Amariah Frost, 1792. The ravages of time and weather have conspired to blur the record, but there is sufficient evidence to establish that these two graves are those of Rev. Amariah Frost and his first wife, Esther Messinger of Wrentham, daughter of the Rev. Henry Messinger. Rev. Frost was to marry again, twice. This is a historically important marker, and it should be preserved and restored.

The Rev. Amariah Frost was the first minister of the "Easterly Precinct" (today's Milford) and of the First Congregational Church. He had served also as a "chaplain in the revolutionary army" and was well acquainted with Gen. Washington. On November 6, 1789, when President Washington stopped in Milford, he "recognized the old gray-headed Puritan Pastor, and greeted him with a burst of cordial affection, exclaiming, 'Why, Old Daddy Frost, is this you?'"

For Decoration Day 1872, Post 22, GAR (Grand Army of the Republic), announced plans to decorate the graves of all soldiers in the cemeteries at North Purchase, Pine Grove, the Catholic and Spruce Street and, for dedication exercises, Vernon Grove.

On October 15, 1874, the *Milford Journal* reported, "A stone erected by the town of Milford over the grave of Rev. Amariah Frost…is still standing in the old burying ground on Spruce Street." That stone, now at Vernon Grove and nearly unreadable, bears the following words:

> *With sacred awe let mortals tread*
> *Where, buried, rest the silent dead;*
> *His virtues known, his name shall last*
> *When rolling moons and suns have past.*

Ballou tells us in his preface that he prepared his *History* between the spring of 1876 and December 1881. The actions of the GAR on Decoration Day 1872, and continuing on through the office of Milford's veterans' agent, show that a new fashion of respect had taken hold toward the cemeteries and the way they were treated, undoubtedly a respect borne of the Civil War. Ballou seems to have recorded a pre–Civil War attitude.

The Rev. Edward A. Perry, pastor of the Universalist Church (1873–78), speaking at Pine Grove, defined the various meanings of the names used to

Slate stones at Vernon Grove Cemetery in increasingly worn condition. *Author's collection.*

designate the resting places of the dead: "Bury means to conceal; grave a place dug in the ground; church-yard is derived from the fact that the dead were formerly buried in and around churches. The Turks call cemeteries 'Cities of Silence'—a very expressive term—but the most beautiful of all names is cemetery, meaning sleeping-place."

Rev. Frost died in 1792, yet some 82 years later, in 1874, his grave seemed to be still intact at Spruce Street. Sometime before 1884, when the cornerstone for Memorial Hall was laid, the Spruce Street cemetery must have ceased as such, and all the graves that remained were removed to Vernon Grove along with their slate markers.

Today, Milford shows a great deal of love and care for its "sleeping-places." Rev. Mr. Frost and Esther are at rest in a fine setting at Vernon Grove. But his slate stone is soon to be lost forever unless it is saved in time. For though his virtues are known, his name shall not last.

Perhaps his old parish could make arrangements to remove the ancient slate, restore it and preserve it inside the church, perhaps in a glass case at the entry. The town has saved lesser items, and I am sure that the trustees of the Vernon Grove Cemetery would see the historical importance of such a gesture.

In its place at the cemetery, a new and permanent marker could be dedicated. A marker that would explain the strange field of frail slate that stands nearby, lonely and lost, against a background of modern, solid stone.

PICTURE PERFECT

Late in March 1944, 31 young women arrived at the Hopedale Community House to participate in a "Capping" there. They were led by Mrs. Lloyd Fitzgerald, their nurse instructor. Representatives from the Red Cross Worcester Chapter were speakers, and Mrs. Fitzgerald received praise for her loyal work and was presented with flowers and a gift from the class. The local Red Cross Volunteer Nurses' Aide committee directed all activities of the nurses' aides and was represented at the meeting with Chairman Mrs. Hamilton Thayer presiding as master of ceremonies.

As a member of this committee and a representative of the medical staff at the Milford Hospital, Dr. Joseph Ashkins spoke a few words, telling the aides how appreciative the doctors are of their work in the hospital. With the awarding of the "Caps," the young women were acknowledged to be "trained to work under the supervision of graduate nurses in the Milford Hospital."

After the ceremonies finished and before the punch and cake were served in the lounge, the class photo, seen on the following page, was arranged and taken. Fifty-six years later, an original copy came my way when I visited Hazel (McNiff) Young and her husband, Merton, at their Wellesley home. Hazel is seen here.

From a photographer's viewpoint, this is an exceptional photo for such a large group. Think of your class reunion photos—even by professionals—and someone has closed eyes or the head in the wrong way. This is a unified group at full attention; it is their photo on their day, and they are the picture of their success.

The 31 members of the Red Cross Volunteer Nurses' Aide Corps who received their caps during ceremonies held at the Hopedale Community House in March 1944 were, left to right: *Top row*: Evelyn Calabrese, Dorothy Prince, Regina Calitri, Poppy Ramelli, Theresa DeCesare, Margaret Meomartino, Christine DeCesare, Evelyn Cenedella, Lois Shea and Cecelia Grant. *Middle row*: Amy Rappazini, Estelle DeManche, Eileen Carney, Ada DiGiannantonio, Sylvia Klem, Eleanor Bird, Anna Heroux, Helen Gaskill, Olga Oneschuk, Rita Norton and Hazel McNiff. *Front row*: Beryl Dawes, Mrs. Clifford Peterson, June Malloy Wright, Angelina Alberto, Mrs. James Piper, Mrs. Lloyd Fitzgerald, RN, Alberta Flaherty, Dorothea Tomasini, Doris Goodnow, Harriet Hall and Roselinda D'Alesio. *Author's collection.*

There is no credit for the photographer. Recent research has led me to think that the Draper Corp. would have sent its photo department to handle the assignment for the Milford Hospital. The names that I remember as Draper photo men were Charlie Shanahan and Bernie E. Norton. I have spoken with Arnold Nealley of Hopedale, and he mentions Andrew Nealley, but I can't connect him to the photo department in 1944.

Hazel and Merton Young were married at St. Mary's by Rev. Joseph Lacey in April 1949. I spoke with their firstborn, Claudia. I had photographed her, in Mendon, where the Youngs had settled. I next saw her at her mother's wake in Wellesley Hills. Her father passed away in April 2013. I am still thankful for the gift of the photo seen here. Claudia has described her mother "as a very special person." That was so true to all of her family and friends.

Many of the people in the photo are now gone, including June (Malloy) Wright, who died in January 2012. I see Poppy Ramelli is still here. I hope that others are, too, and that you can tell us the names of anyone you see. I hope this will be a great memory trip for many.

Author's note: The following notice appeared with the original version of this story. No one was able to name all the young women, but they were all eventually identified, as you can see in the accompanying photo.

Please take a few moments to look over the photograph and see how many of the young nurses' aides you can name. We are giving a prize to the reader who submits the most correct names. If you'd like to enter our contest, please name the nurses' aides, left to right starting with the top row. Remember there are 56 young women. Submit your guess to Jane Bigda, Town Crier *editor, 48 Mechanic St., Upton, MA 01568 or by email to milfordtowncrier@charter.net.*

The deadline for entries is May 4. We will print the names of the nurses' aides and winner of our contest in the May 14 Milford Town Crier. *Good luck!*

Angelina Monica:
"The Greatest Woman I Have Ever Known"

The greatest woman I have ever known, in what by now is a long life, was a second or third cousin of my father's, Angelina."

The late Robert Cenedella, former Milford schoolteacher and Stacy principal (resigning in 1943), wrote these words to me in the mid-1990s when he was still living in New York City, before his retirement and relocation to Tucson, Ariz.

"The greatest woman I have ever known…Angelina." Angelina Cenedella. I had forgotten those words—that letter—and when it surfaced recently, I went looking for Angelina. She was to remain, however, somewhat elusive from my efforts to find her, my desire to learn about this woman whom one old friend was to describe as "saintly."

But I was looking for Angelina Cenedella. Once I learned that I should be seeking Angelina "Monica"—Italian for sister or nun—it was another matter. Doors began to open, and people began to appear who had known Angelina and known her well.

Angelina died in May 1951, and the decades since have removed many of her contemporaries. Three were to be discovered, though, and from the voices of their memories an image of Angelina began to appear. The door of discovery first opened when I met with Michael and Mary Mancini of Central Street, Milford. Both are gone now. The Mancinis had been longtime friends of Angelina, and Michael had served as a bearer when she died.

It was Mary Mancini who was able to "create" Angelina "Monica" for me and to send me off to a meeting in Somerville with a lady who had lived

Left: Angelina Cenedella cutting the cake at her first birthday party when she was 84 years old. *Courtesy of Doc Tessicini.*

with Angelina in the early 1920s as a "state child." And it was Mary who still retained a memory of Angelina as "saintly."

Angelina and her mother, Letizia, arrived from Italy sometime in the year 1900. They settled in the "Plains" and first lived at 117 East Main Street, then moved on to 5 Middleton Street and, finally, to Angelina's last home, the "Stone Castle" at 13 Reade Street. (See "Giovanni Battista Giacomuzzi's 'Stone Castle,'" page 95.)

The 1920 United States census lists Angelina and her mother and, living with them, seven children placed there by the state. Among the children that year was Anna Maria Travaline, age eight. She was Ann MacLeod of Somerville and 84 years young when I spoke with her about Angelina.

Ann had been separated from her siblings when her mother had died and her father could not keep the family together. She was to spend two years with Angelina and to keep a lifelong friendship with her and with Mary Mancini.

It was Ann who was to tell me stories of living with Angelina and how they would sit on the front steps—all the children together—and pray the rosary, but "no speaking." If someone passed by, it was only Angelina who would greet them with "hello." At Christmas, letters were written to Santa Claus, but all requests were for clothes, "no toys." And in the summertime, Angelina would make root beer for them all.

One story is charming but apocryphal. Ann remembers that Angelina would take all the children—just girls at Angelina's—off to confession with

Father Ermino Lona, pastor at Sacred Heart. According to Ann, Father Lona did not speak English, so Angelina would "hear" the confession and repeat it in Italian for Father. What a trial for a child.

Bob Cenedella wrote that "Angelina had scarcely arrived from Italy when she learned of orphans…and she volunteered to take in as many as possible." Angelina made her living as a seamstress and dressmaker, and of course, the state paid her a pittance of sorts. Ann MacLeod thought it was three dollars or so. That was per month.

Elvera (Bregani) Roberti of Purchase Street used to go every afternoon to Angelina's, where she was taught embroidery, and the fee was one dollar per month.

Mrs. Roberti remembered the time when one of the state children, Jenney, was to have her First Communion and had no white dress, etc., to wear. Angelina sent a letter off to the state, and one day, a large box arrived with a communion dress, white shoes, veil—the works.

Angelina has been described as a quiet woman, sad, not jovial and with a soft voice. And she is remembered with love.

Bob Cenedella had written about a party for Angelina that he had heard about, and it was true. It was the first birthday party she ever had, and it was held at Vera Roberti's home on September 21, 1949. Six women joined together to honor Angelina in her 84th year. Many will be remembered although all are gone now: Alma (Barbadoro) Maher; Anna (Mazzerelli) Barra; Anna Frascotti; Josephine (Morcone) DiNardo; and Phyllis DeSantis, foster daughter to Angelina and the "state child" who stayed until the end. In January 1973 she joined Angelina and her mother, Letizia, at Sacred Heart Cemetery. Vera Roberti, who lived to share memories of Angelina with me, joined her friends on April 6, 1998.

They had all given to Angelina a party of love and gratitude in recognition of a woman who was to be remembered by the Sacred Heart parish, some 19 months later, as "one of our most beloved parishioners, a good soul to whom the Church was a second home and her first concern."

Angelina "Monica." "She lived as a nun in the world…and even during her long sickness she always had the smile of a Saint."

I have written of the late beloved Emilio Pighetti that as "an immigrant to these shores, he represented the finest tradition of service to one's community." Could one say any less of Angelina Cenedella? Angelina was a woman of great love, and she gave it all away.

Angelina "Monica" Cenedella was a plain lady of the "Plains." She served "her children," her church and her adopted community and served all with love.

Corner of Main and Central Streets, 1940s. *Author's collection.*

Burns Court and the
Milford Federal

The evolution of a building will take place over time, and Milford has many examples to show the changes that time will bring. As we change with time, so do our surroundings.

The three Milford buildings that composed the Bank Block have changed dramatically over the past 60 years or so. The two taller buildings have had their top floors removed, and the center building has disappeared completely.

The Bank Block for many years was home to the Milford Savings Bank and the Milford National Bank. The top floor was removed in December 1957, and many changes occurred during the next few years.

The Milford National purchased the New England Telephone building at 256 Main Street and Park Terrace—site of the first Davoren's Pharmacy—and built the bank office one can still see today. The telephone company moved all of its operations to its new facilities on Water Street.

With the razing of the third floor at the Milford Savings Bank and the removal of the Milford National to its new building, Milford Savings took over the entire ground floor of the Bank Building. However, Karl Bright Insurance retained an office there until relocating to Congress Street.

Many will recall the offices on the second floor and the staircases up, first in the center at 234 Main and then to the right side of the building. A walk-up would find—in different time periods—Dentist, Dr. Henry Iacovelli; Atty. Daniel J. O'Brien; Judge Chester F. Williams; and Atty. Wendell Williams. John J. DeSalvia, Podiatrist, and Michael J. DeCesare, CPA, had offices there also, as did two longtime residents, Atty. Joseph A. Gattoni and Judge Gordon A. Shaw.

The center building in the photo was known as the Burns Block, and the passageway to the left was known as Burns Court. In an earlier day, it provided access to the stables of George A. Sherborne, teamster and expressman.

Timothy Burns, cigar manufacturer, had purchased the property from the widow of Jesse A. Taft, Esquire, former town solicitor (1892–1905). Mr. Taft had died in October 1905. When Burns acquired the property from Ida Claflin Taft, there was a large house there—where George Sherborne made his home—set back some 20 feet from Main Street. The deed included this provision: "Said premises are hereby conveyed upon the strict condition… that the grantee (Burns)…shall never erect any building…the front line of which shall be nearer said Main Street than would be the front line of the building now erected on the adjoining land of said [Milford] Savings Bank." Burns built to the deed restriction.

On June 8, 1906, the *Milford Daily News* reported that "Waters & Hynes, the local contractors, are to build the two story business block, which Selectman Timothy Burns is to erect on Main Street." Burns served as a selectman from 1906 to 1907. In the 1907 election, after a recount, he was reelected by five votes.

Burns's architect was John F. Sunderland, a graduate of Milford High School in 1897. Although he drew the plans, the project was supervised by local architect Walter L. Collins, as Sunderland was committed to other duties in Philadelphia.

The *Daily News* also reported that "Selectman Burns is having his stable at the rear and the dwelling house removed and converted into double tenement houses." His apartment houses in the rear were sold after his death in 1936, and for a long time one was occupied by the Charles R. and Orrin J. Davis families, until they sold out in 1958. Other occupants were Felix Bessette, Michael Sannicandro and Robert Dumont. Eventually, the homes were razed and parking areas created.

Burns occupied the store at 240 Main Street, where he manufactured and sold his cigars. His next-door tenants, jointly, were Milford Electric Light and Power Co. and the Milford Gas Light Co. Burns lived upstairs at what was then numbered 241. Many will remember the offices of Dr. George S. Nossif there, before he moved to Congress Street.

The Burns Block had many tenants over the years, including, in the early 1950s, both Central Cleaners and the Children's Shop. By 1956, Central Cleaners had moved to South Bow Street and Susan's Children's Wear

Paul Curran (left) and the late Paul Bozzini, president of the Milford Federal Savings & Loan Association, stand by the Burns Court Plaque of Remembrance. Bozzini's leadership was essential to the restoration of Burns Court. *Author's collection.*

would replace it. Karl Bright Insurance would also occupy here temporarily, as would Berardi Loan. Eventually, Susan's would occupy the entire Burns Block and be operated by Rosalie "Babe" Marcus and her husband, Harvey. It was sold to the Milford Federal Bank and razed in 1985. The Bank operations now extended from Franklin Street to Burns Court.

The Milford Co-Operative Bank purchased the Blunt Block from the Milford Savings Bank in November 1935. It was made a federal bank in 1937 and changed to its current name, Milford Federal Savings and Loan Association.

Early postcards show the A.B. Morse Pharmacy located in the Blunt Block at 244 Main Street and Frank E. Withington, grocer, at 246. The pharmacy would become the Park Pharmacy, Mickey Bibbo, pharmacist, and his brother John as clerk. Their future location would be in the Murray Building at Main and South Main. Frank Withington died in 1915. The grocery was operated as the Withington and then moved to Exchange Street. At one time, the First National grocery chain had a store at 246 Main Street.

As we see today, Milford Federal totally absorbed the location, and the memory of Michael Angelo Blunt's building, per se, disappeared. However, many Milfordians will recall visiting the Palace Barber Shop on the second floor, with barbers Mickey DeLuca and Henry Pillarella. Or Dr. Myron Dorenbaum, dentist and golfer. And one of the early tenants, Dr. Sidney M. Heller, chiropodist, who began his Milford practice there on November 12, 1937. And Ann Moia, who operated Ann's Beauty Salon and lived at 55 Franklin Street.

All has changed; the Blunt, Burns and Bank Blocks are one. Milford Federal, from 232 Main Street at South Bow to 246 Main at Franklin Street, is now one bank.

Again, much Milford history has disappeared, but in 1998, the Milford Federal Savings and Loan Association placed a Plaque of Remembrance at its wonderfully restored and saved Burns Court.

The late Paul Bozzini, then bank president, and his Board of Directors should be commended for that gesture and for their continued commitment to Downtown Milford.

Milford Legion ballplayers in their heyday. *Author's collection.*

WENDELL T. PHILLIPS— ATHLETE, ARCHITECT

The 1908 yearbook for Milford High School—the *Oak, Lily and Ivy*—lists 23 graduates that year; the name Wendell T. Phillips does not appear. The name of his future wife, Eva Margaret Smith, does. They were married some six years after her graduation and two years after Wendell Phillips took his degree in architecture at Notre Dame, 1912.

Phillips had left Milford High School—where he had been an outstanding athlete—after his junior year in 1907. In June that year, Phillips and his teammates, "the champion Milford High School baseball team," were given a banquet in their honor. Toastmaster was Thomas J. Murphy, sub-master of the high school and manager of the victorious team.

The *Milford Daily Journal* reported that Murphy offered congratulations and thanks "to all those who helped to make the team a success this year," and went on to speak of the "debt of gratitude the team owed to 'Sime' Hickey, veteran baseball player and coach."

Manager Murphy continued his remarks and spoke of "the regret he had in common with all the scholars at the school at losing such a star athlete as Wendell Phillips," who was scheduled to enter Notre Dame that fall. In April, the *Milford Daily Journal* had reported that Rev. John A. McNamara, Notre Dame graduate and Milfordian, had arranged for Phillips to enter Notre Dame in September.

The paper referred to Phillips as "undoubtedly the best baseball player and pitcher the school ever turned out, but [he] will not graduate from the school until 1908."

On September 9, at the Elks Hall, a private dance and reception was held to honor Wendell Phillips, William J. Moore, William J. Clancy and William E. Curtin, "well known Milford young men, who are shortly to attend colleges." They were, respectively, a future architect, lawyer, dentist and doctor.

Phillips and Moore were to graduate from Notre Dame, and Moore went on to receive his law degree from Boston University. Clancy graduated from Holy Cross and Harvard Dental, and he practiced in Milford. He was also the dentist for the Milford Board of Health. William E. Curtin, captain of the 1907 baseball team, graduated from Baltimore Medical College in 1913. He lived and practiced in Plymouth until his death in 1955.

Wendell Phillips played varsity baseball at Notre Dame for four seasons, 1908–11. During his first season there, he was a member of a team that was called in 1908 "the best ever."

That team won 15 games of their western swing and had six wins in their eastern competition. They had but one defeat that year—a loss to Vermont on May 19.

The next day, Wendell Phillips was scheduled to pitch against Boston College at the South End grounds off Huntington Avenue—the National League ball grounds. A sprained ankle incurred in the Vermont game kept Phillips off the mound and out of the BC game, however.

In spite of the injury, it was to be a memorable day for Phillips. As the *Boston Post* reported:

> *Three hundred Milford baseball fans attended the ball game here yesterday…hoping to see Wendell Phillips, a Milford boy, pitch for the Notre Dame team.*
>
> *They were disappointed as Phillips warmed the bench, unable to go on the firing line…owing to his sprained ankle.*
>
> *Phillips is a great favorite in Milford, having a record of winning every game in which he pitched for the high school team last year, virtually winning the pennant for that school in the Midland series.*

The Milford fans had not only journeyed to Boston to see Phillips pitch, they had also come to honor him. Before the start of the game, Charles J. Smith Jr.—future brother-in-law to Phillips—presented a handsome solid gold watch, chain and charm to the young collegian on behalf of the Milford fans. In presenting the gift, Mr. Smith said:

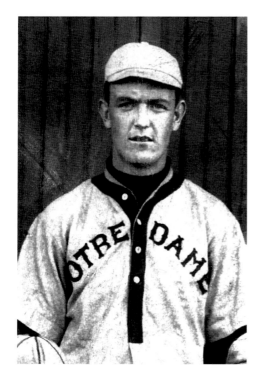

Wendell Phillips played varsity baseball at Notre Dame for four seasons, 1908–11. During his first season there, he was a member of a team that was called in 1908 "the best ever." *Author's collection.*

On behalf of a few of your friends I wish to extend to you our hearty congratulations for the success you have achieved on the baseball diamond and I also desire to express our sincere wish and earnest hope for your future success and prosperity.

Accept this little token as a remembrance of the esteem in which you are held by your friends in the good old town of Milford.

The watch is engraved with the words, "Presented to Wendell T. Phillips by his friends, May 20, 1908."

The *Milford Daily Journal* reported that "the gift came as a great surprise to the college twirler and in a few, well chosen words he thanked Mr. Smith on behalf of the Milford people for the handsome gift."

That was Wednesday. Three days later, on Saturday morning, Wendell Phillips and his Notre Dame teammates were greeted at the White House by President Theodore Roosevelt. The *Milford Daily News* reported that "President Roosevelt gave a 10 minute talk to team members…and…in addition the President shook hands with each member of the college team."

With his degree in architecture from Notre Dame, Wendell Phillips went on to have a productive architectural career. *Author's collection.*

President Roosevelt also inquired of Wendell Phillips the nature of his injuries received in the Vermont game.

Phillips, in a letter to a local friend, stated that he exhibited his new gold watch and that it had been highly admired since he received the gift. The watch today—totally restored and more than 100 years old—is in possession of Wendell T. Phillips of Milford, grandson of the original owner.

THE THOM BUILDING

For a number of years now, I have been in search of James Thom, builder in 1891 of the Thom Building, still extant today at the northeast corner of Main and Spruce Streets. Who was James Thom? I first found mention of him in the *Milford Gazette* of October 1888 when he was a news item as "a foreman at the Pink Granite Company's works and was assaulted with a knife by a workman." The *Gazette* listed him as James Thorne, a mistake that would be repeated in his *New York Times* obituary in July 1926.

Even so, the "obit" made it possible to find his death certificate. James Thom, who died in Brooklyn, N.Y., on July 25, 1926, was born in Scotland in 1850 and came to the U.S. around 1870.

Thom was an early and important promoter in Milford—an early Milford entrepreneur—but a hard man to find. Recently, though, I came across a letter written by Paul Williams, a man with connections to Milford and Mendon, too. He was a great supporter of sporting events. He remembered Thom and tells us a little about him. When the Charles River Driving Park was let go by the Agricultural Society, "the property passed in to the hands of a big, red-whiskered Scotch stone cutter, James Thom. He owned and operated the Park for a decade or more." The Driving Park was a horse-racing track and sports venue on Route 85.

In 1891, the association ran into trouble with Thom over the question of renting his field and moved on to the athletic ball field at the corner of Medway and East Main Streets. Thom, however, was a fighter and

The Thom Building's solid and handsome structure matches the persona of its builder, Scottish stonecutter James Thom, an early Milford entrepreneur. *Author's collection.*

organized a better ball team for the Driving Park. Until it ceased to be a park, it remained the scene of about all of Milford's semi-pro games.

Williams also has revealed another side to Thom's character, one that may have sent him out of Milford in 1893. "Mr. Thom's ambitions in the matter of sports, especially horse racing, were so lofty that in the middle 90s, a bank in St. Johnsbury [Vt.] took possession of the Park as mortgagee."

Thom moved away, but he did leave behind an unusual building that has been a prominent feature downtown for well over a century. It has survived a number of fires—the only building that has endured on the entire stretch of Main Street from Callery Square to Lincoln Square. Gone are the Ideal Theatre, Weber & Rose, Freddy's Music Shop, Tony Gardella's Fruit Stand, Shea Brothers, David Rosen's Law office and, at the end, 133 Main Street, the Crystal Spa.

In July 1891, the *Milford Gazette* reported: "James Thom made arrangements this morning with Norcross Bros., Darling Bros., and the Milford Pink

Memorial Hall, built to honor Civil War soldiers, sits proudly at the corner of Spruce and School Streets. Memorial Hall currently houses the Milford Historical Museum, which contains numerous resources including Civil War artifacts. *Author's collection.*

Granite Co. for polished blocks of stone from their quarries, which will be placed in the northeast corner of his block, thus showing the quality of the stock from the three largest granite industries in town."

They may still be seen today and in prime condition.

At the same time, Thom let it be known that he had decided to place an elaborately carved cornerstone at the corner of his new block. "The stone will be of Milford granite, about six feet square, and will bear a Scotch thistle, the name Thom, and Mr. Thom's own personal coat of arms. The stone will be cut by Mr. Thom himself, who is adept in the art."

The stone is still in place today, but within it, Thom allegedly had placed copies of the local papers and plans of the building, which is the first business block of granite to be built in town, plus other facts of importance. Those items may no longer be inside Thom's "time capsule"—if they ever were—due to subsequent renovations of the building. I am sure that we will find much more to write about James Thom, but for now, I am most gratified to learn that the Thom Building has been on the U.S. National Register of Historic Places since June 23, 1983, and James Thom is listed as the architect.

State Theatre, an ornate two-story movie theatre complete with balcony, was demolished in the 1980s to make way for a bank and parking lot. *Author's collection.*

MILFORD'S
MAIN STREET MALL

Ihave written of an event that occurred more than 65 years ago, the
military funeral of Corp. David Rubenstein, the 24th Milford man to die
in World War II and the first to be brought home for burial (see page 107 for
his story). My account and the cover of this book both feature a memorable
photograph—undoubtedly taken by a young, and soon-to-be-married, Nick
Tosches—of a horse-drawn caisson carrying Rubenstein's flag-covered
coffin up Main Street at Lincoln Square.

Seen behind the cortege that day, and seen more clearly here in
a photograph from October 1959, is an earlier Milford. To many
Milfordians the scene will bring back memories; to younger Milfordians
or newer residents, the scene will be a mystery. The photograph shows
what was there. Today we see what remains. Milford has changed, and
this is but a segment of its time and the people who were in it. Here is an
attempt to remember the buildings but, most importantly, the people of
that long-ago day.

Five buildings on the northeast side of Main Street are all gone now but
one, Thom's Granite Block at Main and Spruce Streets—Callery Square
(see page 143 for a story about the surprising life of James Thom). The
centerpiece of the five buildings, looking east, was the old Arcade Block.
The main attraction, dead center at Lincoln Square, was the Crystal Spa at
133 Main Street, William B. Fokas, Prop. If you didn't go in for a famous hot
dog (gimme the works!), you may have been in the night crowd waiting for
the *Boston Record* to arrive. "Ah, the number, the number!" Originally called

Crystal Lunch, it later moved to 126 Main Street. The Crystal Spa with "Kooch" and "Mina" was a Milford landmark for generations.

At 131 Main was the Lee Frances Beauty Shop, founded by Louise (Lee) Frances Webster—of the Dilla Street Websters—and sold by her sister, Virginia Webster Oneschuk, to Albert Rao of 47 Hayward Street. He continued on at 131 Main. Eventually, that location became Helen's Hat Shoppe, Helen Smith of Forest Street, Prop. Her daughter, Evelyn, was a classmate of mine at St. Mary's, and Helen closed the shop as demolition arrived in the fall of 1959.

Number 129 Main was the stairway up for an assortment of offices, nooks and crannies. Atty. David Rosen (remember the bow ties?) was there, and his name is still seen on the law offices at 35 Main Street. Doris Anne Francesconi, a 1946 graduate of Milford High School, was Dave Rosen's secretary. In June 1952, she would marry Sid Kurlansky, owner of the Atlantic Gas Station that faced School Street at the corner of Spruce Street.

Also back there and facing School Street was Jimmy's Taxi, TEL. 1414—located next to Sharkey's Diner, forerunner of Jean's Catering. Jimmy's was run by the DiSabito brothers, Jimmy and Leo. "Sharkey" was Anthony Ozella.

Directly above the Crystal Spa were the rooms of the Milford Board of Health, a longtime tenant. Also located there was the Milford Chamber of Commerce. The school physician in 1948 for the Board of Health was Dr. John R. Cicchetti, having succeeded Dr. John V. Gallagher upon Gallagher's retirement.

Sharkey's Diner, 1944. Anthony Ozella, amateur boxer and stage manager at Lake Nipmuc, ran the Lincoln Square diner during the '40s and '50s. His left hook earned him the nickname "Sharkey." *Author's collection.*

Throughout the war years and beyond, Alice E. Fitzpatrick, RN, was there—St. Mary's Academy, 1933—at the Board of Health as the parochial school nurse. Helen Breault, RN, served as the Milford public school nurse. The Milford Directory for 1948 lists William J. Clancy as the Board of Health dentist, but he had died in December 1946, and John A. Cleary, DMD, was appointed to the position.

Percy Abel, cigar maker, was upstairs at 129, as was Joseph Kurlansky, also a cigar maker. He was the father of Sidney and also Mrs. David Rosen. But the nooks and crannies of the second floor provided one mystery for me: Alice Marie, Dressmaking—but who was she? I later learned that she was Alice Marie Introini, of 19 Short Street. A lifelong Milford resident, she died in September 1983.

Downstairs at 127 Main was Shea Bros. Market. The brothers had been Dennis and William J. Shea, but in 1948, it was William A. Shea, son of William J. Shea's was a place in my youth where you could call—the phone number was 9—and order fresh meat and produce, which would be delivered to your home. As a young boy, I was there often and fondly remember a kindly Bill Shea.

Next door was "David the Tailor"—David Andreano, uncle of former Tax Collector Bob Andreano and Joanna Gonsalves. Working with Dave over the years were Gennaro and Sammy D'Agostino, uncle and grandfather, respectively, to the VanAlstine family of that time. The VanAlstine women have merged with the Collins, Usher, Oliva and Gallerani families of today's Milford.

Next to David the Tailor was a small doorway that led to the apartments above. This was Scott's Block (old) that ran from Dave's at 125 Main to the Jefferson House, Rooms, at 109.

Alice Foyle, bookkeeper at the former Casey's Hardware Store for more than 35 years, was a longtime tenant at 123 Main Street. Phyllis Ahearn told me that she often watched parades from the open porch or balcony above the business block.

In October 1938, a small ad in the *Milford Daily News* announced the opening of the STORK SHOP, "Infants and Children's Wear," at 121 Main Street, Margaret G. Morcone, Prop. A graduate of Milford High School, Ms. Morcone was also a graduate of the Milford Hospital School of Nursing, 1929.

Number 119 Main Street was empty in 1948, but I will never forget the barber, Jimmy Carron, who later occupied the space for more than a half century. When I was a child, my brothers Ross and Leo decided to give me a little spin in an empty barber chair one day…out I went, crashing; no haircut that day. Today, Tommy Stock continues the family tradition.

Above: A shopper tends to her errands on what was once Milford's bustling Main Street. *Author's collection.*

Below: Maurice J. Tobin, 56th governor of Massachusetts (1945–47), at Cahill's News Agency in downtown Milford to celebrate the capture of a gem thief nabbed in Milford. Tobin created Mass Port Authority and later was appointed secretary of labor under President Truman. In 1967, the Mystic River Bridge was renamed the Tobin Memorial Bridge. *Author's collection.*

And Tony Gardella's Fruit Stand. Remember the roasted peanuts? Tony was assisted by Natale Charles Grillo, "Nate the Worker," Milford High School, 1946. Nate started with Tony when he was 11 and stayed until Uncle Sam called in 1951.

Paul and Doris Charest would open their Chez-Vous Donut Shop at Tony's old location on October 18, 1956. They would move to 192 Main Street, former site of Riseberg's.

Number 113 Main was listed as vacant in 1948, but at 115 was the store of the brothers David and Harry Rubenstein, Rubenstein Electric. Harry was the father of Corp. David Rubenstein. (See "First Hero Home," page 107.)

The same day Corp. Rubenstein's cortege passed through town—April 23, 1948—the *Milford Daily News* ran an ad for the "Grand Opening" of the new MUSIC NOOK, Ed "Slim" Pagnini, Prop. Location was 115A Main Street, where Freddy Imbruno had operated his music shop. The Music Nook, a Main Street musical tradition, is currently operated by the chain Music and Arts, which honors the shop's legendary past by retaining the original sign.

Then came, at 111 Main Street, "Milford's Locksmith," Archie Kalpagian: Locks, Keys, Shoes shined, Hats blocked. How many problems of panic did he solve?

Next door was the entrance to the Jefferson House, Lillian McGonnell, Prop. Tony Gardella lived there and died there on Christmas morning 1952. Mrs. McGonnell was living on Jefferson Street when she died in October 1971. She is buried at the North Purchase Cemetery, as her mother was Ida Morey, a Milford native.

The Arcade Block—sometimes called the "flat-iron" building—and Scott's (old) Block were demolished in the fall of 1959. Eventually, the Werber and Rose location—Scott's (new) Block—would go, as well as the Ideal Theatre location in the Raftery Block. Many people spoke to me with memories of the Ideal. Bob Andreano recalled having 25 cents for a Saturday matinee at the movies. He would spend 12 cents for his ticket and 10 cents for popcorn, and after the show, he would visit the gum machine in front of the Milford Locksmith Store and the remaining pennies would be gone. The Ideal Theatre, how could you forget it or Eleanor Iannetti, MHS '42—the Ideal Theatre ticket seller, today's Mrs. David Guenther?

Milford, I love you.

John F. Kennedy visited Milford twice in the 1950s during his campaigns for the U.S. House of Representatives and for U.S. Senate. Here he's seen hitting Main Street along with local lawyers and members of the VFW in 1952 as he sought the Senate seat he held until he was elected president in 1960. *Author's collection.*

HAPPY HIGH SCHOOL DAYS

A few years ago, I spoke with Margaret (Kearnan) Tolenti, a St. Mary's graduate. I was looking for information about her St. Mary's days. She told me that her 1932 class had issued the first school yearbook, *The Blue Mantle*.

Giancarlo Bon Tempo, a great source of Milford history, showed me a copy of a yearbook that had been produced by the St. Mary's class of 1932, a true historical record. The seniors of 1932 were 15 girls and 15 boys and one popular young lady who was "in fact the only post-graduate."

The yearbook by the class "went to one who has done so much for us and made our path so cheerful. We take pleasure in dedicating this book to Rev. Father Riordan, our good and loyal pastor." The pastor and his two curates, Rev. John P. Donahue and Rev. Francis H. McCullough, are shown in snapshots.

This was an unusual effort for the class of 1932. It was the Great Depression; President Herbert Hoover would soon be gone and President Franklin Roosevelt in the White House. The future after graduation did not look very bright.

On the cover of the 1932 yearbook is a drawing of a lighthouse. "It is used there as a symbol of the teachings of Christ, which guide the soul to the safety of faith and understanding." It was the perfect symbol for St. Mary's Academy.

The boys on the debating team that year included three members of the class of '32: George Trudell, John Burns and Joseph Gallagher. Also seen with the debating team of 1932 is a young future Jesuit, Francis Sweeney.

St. Mary's graduation ushers, 1945. *Left to right, front*: Gloria DePasquale, Josephine Totaro, Alice Luby, Barbara Rooney, Nancy Nash, Marie Maher and Mary Brisson. *Rear*: Jean Barto, Mary Lou van Alstine, Marie Kirley, Eleanor Mulhern, Betty Ann McManus and Patricia Nudd. *Author's collection.*

In 1980, he wrote "A Backward Education" and gave us an idea of the curriculum in the early '30s: "Four years of Latin, of English, of Christian doctrine; three of French; two of history, besides shorter skirmishes with algebra, geometry, chemistry, and physics. It was hard work, it was boring, it was magnificent."

At Commencement exercises on June 17, 1932, Rev. Patrick F. Doyle, former curate at St. Mary's, was the main guest speaker and presented the Bishop O'Leary cup to Joseph E. Gallagher in recognition of St. Mary's victory in the diocesan debates.

In making his presentation, Fr. Doyle humorously remarked that he would present it to one "who has taken nearly everything here tonight except the Town Hall." He referred to Gallagher, who had delivered the valedictory and captured first prize in the elocution contest, the medal for highest scholarship and athletic attainment and a similar award from Sgt. John W. Powers Post, AL.

The 1932 yearbook of St. Mary's closes with the following sentiments:

"Yet, Ah! That Youth's Sweet Scented Manuscript Should Close." In future years, perhaps, as we chance upon this book and glance through its pages, so long forgotten, we may recall familiar faces and long recollections of our happy years at dear St. Mary's. If this manuscript serve the happy purpose of reviving fond memories, then well may we cherish it as a treasured souvenir, a priceless relic of our happy high school days.

Enjoying being together at the Brass Rail in downtown Milford were, *left to right*: Lt. Joseph R. Manella, Sgt. Cesidio Schiappucci, Lt. George Trudell, Staff Sgt. Fred Moran and restaurant owner Albert "Peck" Macchi. *Author's collection.*

View of Draper Park, 1938, which looks remarkably empty without its war memorials. *Author's collection.*

BIBLIOGRAPHY

Ballou, Adin. *History of Milford, Milford, Worcester County, Massachusetts, from Its First Settlement to 1881*. Boston: Rand and Avery, 1882.

Beyer, Kenneth M. *Q-Ships versus U-Boats: America's Secret Project*. Annapolis, MD: Naval Institute Press, 1999.

Cenedella, Robert. "A Lesson in Civics [Town Meeting]." *American Heritage* 12, no. 1 (1960): 42–43, 100–2.

Garrison, Dee. *Apostles of Culture: The Public Librarian and American Society, 1876–1920*. New York: MacMillan and Co., 1977.

Hopper, Gordon. "The First Cemetery in Milford." Hopper on History, *Milford Daily News*, November 5, 1994, 11.

Milford Historical Commission. *History of Milford 1780–1980*. Milford, MA: 1980.

Petrie, George. *Ecclesiastical Architecture of Ireland: An Essay on the Origins of Round Towers in Ireland*. Dublin: Hodges & Smith, 1845.

Piper, Watty. *The Little Engine that Could*. New York: Platt & Monk, 1930.

Rider, Fremont. *Melvil Dewey*. Chicago: American Library Association, 1944.

Stokes, Margaret. *Early Christian Architecture in Ireland*. London: G. Bell & Sons, 1878.

ABOUT THE AUTHOR

Paul Curran is a native of Milford, Ma., and a graduate of St. Mary's High School class of 1947. He joined the U.S. Army in 1951 and served as an Army photographer and interviewer throughout the Korean War. He later worked as a photojournalist for the *New York Daily News* and as a studio photographer for Bert Stern. Curran returned to Ma. in the 1970s, graduated *magna cum laude* from Framingham State College and developed an interest in local history and

Photo by Kathleen Culler.

local libraries as community resources. He served as an elected trustee of the Milford Town Library for 18 years and was co-chair of the committee that brought a new library to Milford in 1986. He is currently trustee emeritus, and the library's historical research and collections room has been named in his honor. Curran has been a regular columnist for the *Milford Daily News* and the *Milford Town Crier*.